Ronnie Knox Mawer grew up in Wrexham, Wales. During the Second World War he was in the Royal Artillery and then read law at Emmanuel College, Cambridge. After being called to the Bar, he joined HM Overseas Judiciary until 1971. He was then on the London Bench until he retired to devote time to writing and occasional broadcasting. His earlier books are Palm Court, Tales from a Palm Court, Tales of a man called Father, A case of Bananas, and Land of My Father. He has written for Punch, Argosy, The Listener, The Times, Telegraph and Independent. He and his wife June, the broadcaster and prize-winning author, divide their time between Wales and London. They have a son, daughter and grandaughter Polly.

By the same author

ARE YOU COMING OR GOING?

My sixty years on the run

by Ronnie Knox Mawer

For dear Pat, who is doing fine, despite the gremlins, with special love. (Hope to raise an occasional smile.)

Ronnie 23.12.99.

Illustrations by Graham Kennedy

Holiday Books

ISBN 0 9535481 0 4

Reproduced, printed and bound in Great Britain by
WBC Book Manufacturers Ltd
Bridgend, Mid Glamorgan,
Wales

Published 1999 by Holiday Books
Plas-yn-Bonwm, Corwen,
Denbighshire LL21 9EG
Telephone/Fax (01490) 413019

Contents

CHAPTER ONE

ARE YOU COMING OR GOING?

"Are you coming or going?"   At home in Wales, it was a question regularly fired at me by my huge and terrifying Father whenever I took a breather from his iron regime of daily tasks and duties. These multiplied with the coming of World War Two. I seemed to be forever waiting to be told what to do next. A condition that has shaped my life ever since.

Back in the nineteen-thirties Miss Einwen Pritchard, the dragon of Acton Park Primary, had goaded me along. Her classroom techniques of punishment and reward finally propelled me into Grove Park Grammar School. There, despite my ingrained timidity, I was dangerously miscast as a rugby-forward on account of my lanky physique. Only after a series of missed kicks and fumbled passes were my services terminated.

As time went by I seemed to make a habit of finding myself in unsuitable positions. The Army, for instance, had me in mind as a Heavy Duty Driver. This was how I found myself lost in a dense fog en route for Larkhill Barracks, Salisbury Plain. I was at the wheel of a 3-ton truck unequipped with synchromesh gears. Hence the collision into Stonehenge. I was moved swiftly across the Channel under the corrective care of R.S.M. "Tiger" Gogerty, ex-heavy weight champion of the Royal Regiment of Artillery. He dispatched me up a solitary watchtower in the Low Countries to spy upon V 2 Rockets. But apparently I made so little impact upon the authorities that they forgot to tell me to come down though the war had been over for some time. Indeed I might have remained aloft indefinitely had it not been discovered that my name was missing from the Demobilisation List.

Even when, a civilian once more, I eventually qualified in the law, it appeared that fate had a bizarre future mapped out for me. I had certainly not expected to spend my thirty-fifth birthday locked in the embrace of a twenty stone South Sea Monarch at the ritual Dance-Of-Welcome for the visiting judge. The scene of this unhappy episode was the bamboo palace of the reigning King of The Savage Isles, whose ancestors had ceded his Kingdom to Queen Victoria. This had meant exchanging Club Law for English Common Law. A debatable swap for any respectable Savage Islander whose prestige depended upon eating his enemies dispatched by the club. It was, of course, part of the bargain that Whitehall would send a judge to the South Seas, and I was the last of the line.

On the face of things, I did not think it reasonable for H.M.G. to require me to carry with me on those journeys around the Pacific Circuit the complete set of Halsburys Laws of England. Even the lightweight travelling-edition numbered forty-two volumes, stretching every corner of my giant Kitchener Safari Shoulder-Pack. This made for difficulties especially when the weather was unreliable. It was hardly my fault that I encountered one after the other a sharp hurricane in Valva-Lava, a minor earthquake on the Vatuan archipelago, and an electric storm over the New Orkneys. This Island Hopping on my part along the fringes of empire, from one Palm Court to the next, meant a continuing life of no fixed abode. Colleagues back home expressed bewilderment. Where was my lotus-eating existence going to lead?

On to the London Bench as it turned out. In fact my judicial title of "Floater" might have been invented for me. As an extra Stipendiary Magistrate, I was once again on the move, travelling from one Dickensian courtroom to another, at the mercy of the murky tides of Metropolitan Crime. I was hoping for some sort of try-out as a Deputy Judge in the Inner London Crown Court, but a bureaucratic error found me presiding over an Immigration Appeals Tribunal which brought me face to face with my old enemy, Pastor Isiah Mosese, the defrocked serial bigamist of Waikikila.

Although I am now retired to a mountain cottage in Wales I am still the proverbial rolling stone, lurching out in a decrepit Russian Lada along the valleys, pausing to jot down in the local cafes some account of my wayward life. Not surprisingly this is turning out to be more of a scrapbook than a memoir, scenes from A Life On The Run, so to speak.

And as regards Father's question "Are you coming or going?" I leave it to the reader to decide. Is my chronic state of indecision a fatal flaw in character, or have I simply been a victim of circumstance?

All I appear to have done is to describe a complete circle, from Wales and back again.
Perhaps even now I had better keep my options open. Just in case I need to decamp once more.

CHAPTER TWO

SENTENCED TO WALES

The opening months of the last war have generally been regarded by historians as uneventful. This was certainly not the case for those of us living under Father's roof at 26 Grosvenor Road, Wrexham, or Rest Haven as it was inappropriately called. September 3rd had already been ringed in red upon the Pharmaceutical Calendar with the words AT WAR inscribed below. We four children, my three sisters and I, awaited developments in some trepidation.

"I've said we'll take five, Clara," Father announced at lunch on Day Two of Hostilities.

"Five what, dear?"

"Five evacuees from Liverpool."

Father consulted his silver watch kept in the pocket of his outsize waistcoat.

"They should be here within the hour."

This was the first intimation of any kind that Mother had received on the subject.

"We could perhaps manage two, George, but where on earth would five of them sleep?"

"In the guest wing of course."

We had no guest wing. Like so many other things in life such luxuries were a figment of Father's imagination.

Our gaunt Victorian villa was already fully occupied by we four children. In addition I had Stacey Williams, Father's apprentice, taking up three-quarters of my own boxed-in garret at the end of the landing. The first floor was naturally dominated by Father's aptly named Master Bedroom at the front of the house. Through this door he emerged daily at 6 a.m. in a freshly starched wing-collar, glaring down at the world through steel-rimmed spectacles.

By doubling up in the other rooms, the rest of us somehow found space for four of the visitors, but Douglas Stannard, a very large fifteen year old from Bootle, had to be escorted by Father up the back stairs to the attic. This bleak outpost had been crammed by Father with discarded bee-keeping equipment.

"If you think my Dougie is going to spend the night in a bloody beehive, you'd better think again" said his mother who had accompanied the hapless adolescent. Unlike the other parents, she had insisted on a tour of inspection. Without another word, the lady gathered her offspring and swept out of Resthaven to find more suitable accommodation. This left a ginger-haired boy called John Hatton, his bespectacled brother Arthur and a pair of small sisters, Mary and Dorothy Holmes, to settle down as best they could into Father's EMERGENCY REGIME. All were from respectable Liverpool schools, like Quarry Bank and Calder High, and were used to discipline. Within days they had become, in Father's words, "very useful as a supplementary workforce."

Their first task was to collect the free government propaganda notices given out at the Guild Hall. Father had them take some to his pharmacy at 9 High Street. Under the poster IT'S YOUR NATIONAL DUTY TO KEEP WELL, pasted on the pharmacy window, the evacuees were instructed to set out a large quantity of unsold stock - mainly liver pills, haemorrhoid ointments and corn plasters. On the opposite side, under the poster ESSENTIAL STEPS IN FIRST AID, the new recruits were set the task of building up a pyramid of shop-soiled bandages topped by Father's Special GARGLE MIXTURE.

Still under Father's supervision, the evacuees joined the rest of the family in bill-boarding at Resthaven. With the aid of a step ladder, we managed to pin onto the kitchen door the directive GIVE YOUR DIGESTION AN EVENING OFF BY SCALING DOWN ON RATIONS. The Hatton boys were then sent down to the Guild Hall for another copy, which was pasted up by the dining-room table as an extra reminder. There was no question of an Evening Off for the workforce at Resthaven. When we did pause for tea, Father arrived home unexpectedly, to find us all "stuffing ourselves with cake" as he put it.

"War means War Rations, Clara" he snapped.

He was only mollified when Mother managed to produce an eggless Victoria Sponge for the weekend, leaving Father's supply of home-grown duck eggs (which we hated) safely reserved for his breakfasts.

Prior to Christmas 1939, gas attacks were anticipated.

So overnight Father decreed that all eight of us children should wear our gas masks wherever possible. As senior Air Raid Warden, he took it upon himself to set the example.

"Must get accustomed to wearing the full respirator,. Clara. While getting on with other things, of course."

During our daily Emergency Practice, Father would don an extra piece of equipment - a strange black helmet captured by Great Uncle Albert from the Austrian Army in 1914.

"For the protection of the head against flying shrapnel" was Father's explanation. Worn with complete breathing apparatus, his appearance was remarkable. Why he should have chosen to prune the damson tree whilst attired in this was never explained.

Surfacing above the wall dividing our garden, number 26, from that of number 28, Father looked startlingly like the scientist in the horror movie THE FLY who had acquired the head of a giant bluebottle.

At the time, our neighbour, Mrs Hurford-Jenkins, was peacefully weeding their bed of African Marigolds. Her shriek of terror rang down the entire road as she was helped into the house. Inevitably her husband, Major Hurford-Jenkins, hurried round to complain.

"Are you trying to win your own War of Nerves, Knox Mawer?!" he demanded. Since Father's voice was muffled behind his mask, the major received no satisfactory reply. Hostilities between the two households was a long established tradition, with both sides equally matched. On this occasion the major notched up a clear victory and Father did not continue with this particular exercise. Instead he turned his attention to me.

"Where's that boy, Clara?"

I reported for duty along with the two Hattons.

"You three can finish off the sandbagging," Father directed.

It was laundry day at Resthaven and we had yet to erect the bulging sacks around the washhouse window.

"Suffocating in there I'll be," complained Miss Carrie Rogers, whose job it was to tackle the weekly mountain of family linen and underwear.

"All you need to do, Miss Rogers, is leave the door open," Father responded as he left us to our task.

A squat, pugnacious figure whom we were allowed to call Aunt Carrie, Miss Rogers was then the only member of the household who resisted Father's Call to the Flag. "We'll never beat them Germans" was her observation repeated in a hoarse whisper behind his back.

She once borrowed a little bakelite receiver and hid it behind the mangle in the washhouse, specially for hearing Lord Haw Haw's broadcast from Radio Bremen.

Mary Holmes and her sister were invited to sit in on this exciting session. It was lucky that Father never discovered what was going on.

"The Tower of London is the only place for people who listen to 'Germany Calling,' Clara," he frequently declared.

Whether or not the Holmes girls took much notice of what was broadcast is doubtful. But, in any case, despite Lord Haw Haw's dire warnings of things to come, they went home for Christmas and did not return afterwards.

The winter turned into Spring and John Hatton and I were bidden to post up another large Government Poster on the garage gates. SAVE VITAL SUPPLIES it read.

"If we're going to pay adequate regard to that particular notice, Clara," Father announced after Sunday lunch "then I think I have the answer."

"How do you mean dear?" asked Mother. We six children turned attentively.

"At Resthaven, summertime will be regarded as having started two weeks early this year."

"How exactly would that help, George?"

"Perfectly obvious!   Summertime is when the coal fires can be left unlit thereby saving fuel for a start!"

Even Father's decree could not be extended to the clocks, but the calendar on the kitchen wall was suitably amended in Father's maroon ink.

Simultaneously the weather took a turn for the worse and the wheezing chest of the older Hatton youth resounded from the next bed as he wrote his weekly letter home. Soon afterwards, an indignant Mr. Hatton came driving over from Toxteth to remove his offspring.

"'I'm going to complain to the Authorities," he said. "Evacuated to *safety* in Wales for heaven' sake! Worse than a prison sentence!"

The rest of us were left to shiver it out as best we could.

Father himself was able to keep up his energy with Masonic dinners, which had now been resumed. He was returning from one of these occasions through our front gate just as Major Hurford-Jenkins was taking his black daschund for an evening walk.

Unhappily, Father's boot collided with the dog. Not surprisingly this caused it to snap back in retaliation.

"If you must walk that German beast after dark, Jenkins, then it should be in your own garden," exploded Father.

"May I point out, Knox Mawer, that my dog is wearing the luminous harness specially authorised by the manufacturers for use in the blackout."

The major returned home and Father retreated to the safety of our entrance hall.

"Just look at this, Clara," he called, pointing to the beast's toothmark in the left leg of his evening trousers.

"Don't worry dear," soothed Mother "I'm sure I can do some invisible mending."

Calming down Father was always a prior necessity and his blood pressure had become dangerously high. She glanced at the clock. "It's coming up to 9 p.m. George," Mother said. I caught her glance and tuned into the BBC News.

The announcer's voice was grave and we fell silent.

"Despite the gallantry of the Dutch and Belgian Armed Forces," he told us "Hitler's Panzer Divisions have swept all before them. The French Government led by Marshall Petain has asked for peace terms."

What had become known as the Phoney War was phoney no longer.

Frowning severely, Father's reaction was to signal for me to switch off the wireless. He next took out a small notebook from his pocket along with his Swan propelling pencil.

"I am instructing my solicitors, Clara. To take immediate action."

We looked at one another.

Was Father planning on taking Herr Hitler to court?   Perhaps the war would not last long after all.

Our delusions were quickly corrected.

"Jenkins will receive from my lawyers three demands, Clara," Father said.

"Firstly he will apologise for the incident in writing. Secondly, he will pay for the repair of my trousers. Thirdly, he must undertake to walk his wretched hound strictly within his own boundaries, upon penalty of a summons for breaching the Black Out Regulations. Clearly that ridiculous paraphernalia in which he encases the animal is totally inadequate."

Father put away his propelling pencil. "Let's see how he likes that!"

Hitler's blitzkrieg was almost over. Father's had only that moment begun.

CHAPTER THREE

A BRUSH WITH THE BBC

Whenever Father was using the telephone at Resthaven, all movement in the house was prohibited. I was standing transfixed outside the downstairs cloakroom while he was speaking on the line to the secretary of the North Wales Chemist's Association, of which he was President.

"I've arranged for the annual meeting to be held on Saturday June 30th at the Masonic Hall," he was saying.

There was a pause, then an explosion.

"No. No. NO! Of course you don't have to be a Mason to get in. The hall is open to any respectable organisation. Naturally since I myself am a Grand Officer in the Masonic Order, it is a simple matter for me to make the booking."

Another explosion.

"Travel problems?! It's precisely because of wartime travel restrictions that Bangor is the most convenient venue, being on the Holyhead line where regular trains continue from both directions."

There was a pause.

"Yes, yes," Father snapped "I know very well that our secretary has joined the Wrens, and we do not have her replacement yet."

He glanced doubtfully in my direction.

"I suppose I could bring this boy of mine along as a very poor substitute. He could at least sharpen the pencils and distribute the agenda sheets."

Because of the wartime petrol shortage, Father had laid up the car which was now mouldering into an even greater state of decay on the damp side of the garage.

"We'd best take the Crosville bus to Chester General" he decided.

Always excessively prompt, his choice of bus and then rail transport landed us outside the Masonic Hall, Bangor, two hours before the meeting was due to start.

"What the devil's going on here?" Father demanded of nobody in particular. From a large van marked BBC, people all around us were carrying microphones and other equipment into the Masonic Hall.

A gentleman in a bow tie and goatee beard who seemed to be in charge stood out in the melee. Father approached him briskly.

"I don't object to giving a brief statement about our work On Air" he said "although the pharmaceutical meeting, as such, is a strictly private affair."

"We happen to be getting ready for the Billy Cotton Band Show, sir," replied the bearded official.

Taken aback Father played for time.

"I'm not acquainted with Mr. Cotton or his show," he said "but in any case the Priority Booking of this building is in my hands."

"I'm sorry to disappoint you sir," came the response "but the BBC has been evacuated from London to Bangor, and these premises are commandeered for our exclusive use."

Father was left to contemplate his next move when a bespectacled figure, wearing a tag marked Studio Manager, arrived on the scene.

"Billy Cotton's now decided to use Penrhyn Hall instead" he told the group of BBC engineers.

He tucked a pencil behind his ear and disappeared inside.

"Mind your back sir" he called out to Father, emerging in the company of Billy Cotton's double bass player. Between them they were carrying the double bass. With a loud twang, Father's umbrella caught against the nearest string.

"You'd be better over here, Mr. Knox-Mawer" interrupted a voice which Father recognised.

It was Mr. Idris Thomas, the Dolgellau pharmacist, and Treasurer of the Association. "Looks as though we're out of luck today," he said. "After all the BBC is somebody. Has to come first. Playing such a vital role in the war effort and so forth."

"And what about the Vital Role played by Number 9, High Street, Wrexham?" Father wanted to know.

A prolonged argument ensued, but eventually Mr. Thomas persuaded Father to calm down over coffee in the adjoining Kardomah Cafe. With Mr. Thomas acting as go-between, a compromise was negotiated.

"So long as you can get your pharmaceutical business over in one hour flat sir, I can guarantee no interruption whatsoever" promised the BBC's representative.

Father duly called his meeting to order.

"Item (a) in the Agenda" he began "Shortage of Essential Medicaments."

Several pharmacists wished to be heard on this subject.

"Take Steradents to begin with" complained Mr. Eifion Jones from Llanrwst, "not a drop available in the whole of the Conwy Valley."

"Tell 'em to manage without, Eifion" piped up Mr. Ivan Jenkins of Prestatyn.

"This is a highly important matter I'm raising, Ivan" persisted Mr. Jones, "in Llanrwst practically the whole of the Home Guard wear dentures."

Discussion on this and other urgent topics seemed to me to last forever, as I hurried about endlessly refilling teacups. Argument raged so noisily that none of the pharmacists noticed that the BBC rehearsal for the Saturday Night Play GASLIGHT had begun at the other end of the Assembly Room.

"Are you the sound effects team?" inquired the Gaslight Producer, confounded no doubt by the appearance of our secretary Mr. Thomas.

Mr. Thomas was wearing a cumbersome Deaf Aid plugged into both ears, while absent-mindedly holding in his hand an empty tea tray, exactly the sort of tray used in radio productions to simulate thunder.

"Do we look as though we've nothing better to do with our time than to make NOISES OFF?" snapped Father. whose amateur theatrical days had ended in 1928 with a disastrous production of THE BELLS at the Wrexham YMCA. He swept up his papers and, with me trailing behind, made as dignified an exit as circumstances permitted.

"Of course it was this boy's fault, Clara," he complained once we were back home "fumbling about with those refreshments. Delayed everything. Made it quite impossible for me to wind things up on time."

"Maybe we're all of us a bit slow adjusting to things just now, George," Mother said. "After all the whole nation is grateful for the BBC these days."

"I'm as keen as the next man for the broadcasting to continue, Clara," Father insisted. "In fact now that the BBC is near at hand in Bangor, I shall be able to give them a few useful suggestions myself."

We looked at one another in bewilderment. What particular role in the field of Wireless Communications did Father have in mind for himself?

"See if that boy can find the wavelength of THE FORCES PROGRAMME" he directed.

From time immemorial, our set had been tuned solemnly into the National Service.

Over on the Forces Programme however, the SWINGING SWEETHEARTS were followed by the CRACKERJACKS. After that, Victor Sylvester "explored the reverse wave in the slow fox-trot at the BBC Dancing Club."

Father listened impassively.

"And now ladies and gentlemen" said the announcer "we go over to hear more laughter from that loveable North Country family, The Plums."

"Family life, Clara" Father remarked with approval "Something along our own lines there I'd say."

Reflected in the mirror above the dining-room fireplace could be seen the four pallid faces of Father's offspring, peering anxiously in his direction. No doubt, to Mother's fond gaze, we were more or less loveable, but it was hard to imagine Father in the role of the genial Mr. Plum.

More music followed.

"Turn up the volume" I was instructed, when Big Ben Campbell and the Rocky Canadian Redwoods began their "yodelling song" accompanied by the Bunk House Boys from their Cabin In The Hills.

"Rousing stuff" Father reflected, making a note in his Druggists Diary.

At that point, he picked up the Radio Times.

"Where in the name of thunder are my reading spectacles Clara?" he demanded.

"They are on your nose dear."

We sat in silence while Father perused the pages of the RT.

"I see they've got some fellow broadcasting as The Radio Doctor, Clara" he remarked. Father's opinion of doctors as "illiterate prescription writers and diagnostic disasters" was well known.

"I'm a busy man these days, Clara, as you well know. However I would be prepared to pop over to Bangor on a weekly basis as The Radio Chemist. Far more important that the average citizen should know what to do about simple complaints like varicose veins and piles."

Unhappily, Father's letter to the Director General received a polite refusal. He was not to become, like J.B. Priestley, the purveyor of nationwide fireside chats.

He retaliated by doing without the BBC for a spell.

"Have that wireless set taken out to the kitchen" we were told.

Aunt Carrie was quick to make use of it. Father little guessed that Lord Haw Haw's subversive broadcasts, from Bremen, were her fascinated listening whenever, as now, she got the chance. And this time my sisters and I could join in this seditious activity. We could be quite sure that the back kitchen was the one room Father never deigned to enter, even in wartime.

CHAPTER FOUR

FATHER'S WARTIME SECRETS

"Say not the struggle nought availeth, Clara" Father announced.

It was 1941, the darkest year of the war. Father had taken to repeating the rhetoric of Winston Churchill. It was Father's duty, as he saw it, to set an example in keeping up the morale in the Wrexham area.

Father was standing in front of the sideboard mirror, removing from his neck a couple of bee stings, acquired upon his latest visit to the hives.

"Can't I help you with that, George?"

He shook his obstinate head.

"The labour and the wounds are vain" he continued, quoting the second line of the poem recently addressed to the nation by the Prime Minister.

Father was now applying a strong carbolic poultice.

"In front the sun climbs slow, how slowly! But westward look the land is bright!"

"What exactly do you mean dear?" asked Mother, taking away the enamel bowl and cotton wool.

Father had moved to the French window and was pointing roughly westwards toward the rooftops of the houses on the opposite side of Grosvenor Road.

"The Ruabon Mountain, for heaven's sake, Clara."

We children looked up at each other across our homework books. We had long given up any attempt to follow Father's thoughts.

"Such an obvious place for the beehives to be sited, Clara! Now that the summer flowers are over I can go further to help the War Effort by obtaining a late-in-the-season supply of mountain heather honey. Inspiration strikes when least expected."

That, strangely enough, was the last we heard from Father of this particular bolt from the blue. Nor would we have heard about it from anyone else, had it not been for a report by Auntie Carrie when she next arrived to take charge of the Monday Washing.

"No wonder Mr. Knox Mawer's never told you anything about it" she said, thudding down a

heavy flat iron upon Father's evening shirt.

"How do you mean, Miss Rogers?" asked Mother. She sounded anxious.

"Took a trip on to Ruabon Mountain, didn't he? Went there with Mr. Jones's bus he did."

"Did he?"

Aunt Carrie was a regular passenger with Mr. "Why Walk" Jones as he was known -WHY WALK WHEN YOU CAN RIDE WITH ME being his famous advertisement in the Wrexham Leader. The motor service he provided ran throughout the district, including Ruabon Mountain, where Aunt Carrie's cousin had a cottage.

"There's them Polish soldiers working up there. Which is how he got arrested as a German Spy."

She paused, relishing the effect of these devastating last words. Mother sank into the nearest chair, holding Father's pile of outsize starched collars in her arms.

"What on earth are you talking about, Miss Rogers?"

"Well the Poles was clearing the ground for the new searchlight on top. Three nights running there's been German planes above. So what do you expect the soldiers to think when they saw this funny-looking man come our of the bushes with his measuring tape and binoculars? Wearing that big bowler of his..."

"But didn't Father *tell* them Auntie Carrie" I began "I mean about the bees and the honey and..."

"Your Father doesn't speak Polish and they didn't understand English. What with all the warnings of enemy agents they thought it was best to be on the safe side. The Polish sergeant marched him off at gunpoint."

The idea of Father intent on a Patriotic Scheme to increase food production only to be taken prisoner, was too much for the rest of us. But Mother hastily quelled our explosions of mirth.

"Goodness me, Miss Rogers. What happened then?"

Aunt Carrie slowly folded a white tie with waistcoat.

"I'm not exactly sure, Mrs Mawer" she prevaricated "although I'm told it all got sorted out at the police station. Not that Mr Knox Mawer would be in the best of tempers about it would he?"

We had no answer to that one, and Aunt Carrie went on.

"I only heard about it on that old bus. You know what gossips they are in them parts."

Obviously it had been an episode in his life that Father had decided should remain closed, and of course Mother was far too sensible to raise the subject.

In any case, his energy was quickly diverted to another project within a matter of hours.

He had pushed aside his breakfast-cup and opened out The Times with a crack like a starting pistol. He had evidently seen something to alert him. We braced ourselves for the next Big Idea.

"I see the Royal Air Force is in urgent need of Trained Carrier Pigeons, Clara" he said. He was peering through his steel-rimmed glasses at a prominent announcement on the centre page. "Vital for life saving purposes it says. Apparently the birds will home from planes in the sea so that the crew can be located. They want Pigeon Fanciers to enrol."

"Do they dear?"

"So I shall send in my name at once."

"But George, you don't have any pigeons. And it isn't anything you..."

Father held up his head.

"You may not know, you children" he said turning to address the rest of the table, "as a boy I had a tame jackdaw. He used to sit on my shoulder and accompany me to school every day. Knew every word I said to him. Made clear to me that I have something of a knack with our feathered friends. You remember the chickens we had last year?"

We looked down at our plates. We remembered only too well. Especially the day they escaped and laid eggs in the back of Major Hurford Jenkins' Morris 10. Father had promptly donated the Rhode Island Reds to the Worshipful Master of the Square and Compass Lodge. "Fine hens, Brother Thorne," we had heard him explain.

"But pigeons dear" Mother tried again.

"But nothing. There's no time to lose. First thing I have to do is arrange for their comfortable accommodation."

For a moment we had a vision of them occupying what Father called The Guest Wing. However, within three weeks, an extraordinary edifice had been constructed along the full length of the rhubarb patch with the ten-foot high garden wall behind for support.

"Naturally" Father explained, taking Dr. Brock upon a conducted tour, "in view of the war-time shortages, building materials and so on, the gardeners have had to make do with the best they can."

In fact Father's gardeners consisted of two conscripts from the Pharmacy- Eric Williams, a pale and weedy individual recently retired from the Photographic Dark Room, and the delivery man Herbert, exempted from Army Service on account of his wooden leg. Together they had made ingenious use of a large number of packing cases with rusty wire netting. A series of rickety steps led from one level to another. The structure had three storeys linked together with what Father called the "landing platform".

"Hold the ladder firmly" he instructed the surprised Dr. Brock, who had merely called in to check on my sister's whooping-cough. "I want you to see for yourself the excellent breeding compartments."

Dr. Brock consulted his watch.

"Only wish I could spare the time" he said "but I'm afraid I'm already late for afternoon surgery."

"I was rather hoping to show you the Granary as well" Father explained as Dr. Brock got into his motor.

"Altogether a most patriotic exercise" commended the doctor. "And please don't forget to take your blood pressure pills this time."

"Blood pressure pills indeed!" Father uttered as he strode indoors to summon Mother outside, to view "progress."

"As you see, I've laid in a good stock of corn in the Granary. For feeding purposes." he said.

"Very good dear" Mother said "but how about the birds?"

"The stock, you mean" corrected Father "no difficulty. I've already made enquiries. Just a question of careful selection."

"Where will they come from George?"

Father waved an expansive arm. "Pentre Broughton, Rhos, Llay, all the miners have their lofts."

Mother look worried. In his own particular field of expertise - pharmaceutical medicine - she was confident that Father could make a worthwhile contribution to the War Effort. But Father seemed to be totally ignoring the fact that he knew nothing about pigeons. The piece in The Times was his only source of information.

"What the Royal Air Force needs, Clara, are breeds with stamina. It's merely a question of having an eye for class. The Aga Khan never seems to have any problems."

"But the Aga Khan breeds racehorses, George."

"Nothing to do with it" was Father's reply.

War-time petrol rationing meant that in order to acquire his racing stable, Father had to make use of public transport. So "Why Walk" Jones's service through the pit-villages was the only answer.

"You can't bring those on here, sir" protested Mr. Dai Jones, Why Walk's bus conductor. Father had just completed a buying spree in Llay. Our large wicker basket was crammed with Father's purchases. He turned to me, his hapless assistant.

"Show the man our tickets" Father told me. Upon his instruction, I had bought one adult, one child and one goods fare.

"Pigeons don't count as goods, sir."

By this time, Father's face had turned an ominous purple. Luckily the rest of the passengers weighed in upon his side.

"Why not let them travel as pets, Dai" somebody called out.

"Of course" Father nodded approvingly "this boy's exceedingly fond of them."

I managed a feeble nod. After two hours of pigeon-handling, while Father blustered his way from one fancier to another, I had already seen quite enough of these particular "pets."

"Go on Dai! You allowed Mrs Llewellyn to bring two ducks on her lap for market without making such a fuss."

"But that was livestock" pointed out the conductor. He had a small black moustache like Hitler.

From inside the basket there came a sound of violent rustling as the lid was forced from one side. The next moment one of the pigeons made an escape and flew up against the wire that rang the bell. With a roar, the driver started off the vehicle and we lurched down the hill towards Wrexham.

"Well that one's live alright Dai" pointed out an old lady in the back. "Who needs you on the bus, with a bird like that!"

It was at school next morning that I was accosted by Evan Jones of Form 3A2 who happened to come from Llay.

"Heard your dad's been buying pigeons in the village" he said. "My uncle says they were having a right laugh about him in the pub last night. He's new at the game isn't he?   Wouldn't know they've palmed him off with a whole basket of non-starters."

Instinctively I rose to Father's defence. "He's been guaranteed that each one is a pedigree," I insisted.

"Then he must be dafter than you, Knoxy."

Aunt Carrie was ironing Father's shirt front for the Bromfield Lodge that evening when I related what Evan Jones had said.

"You'd better not let your Father know" she warned.

There was no need. All too soon he found out for himself the shortcomings of his purchases. They did nothing but eat his food and refused to fly.

As I cleaned up with brush and bucket (another of my regular Saturday tasks) I watched fascinated at the spectacle of fellow creatures resistant even to Father's discipline.

"Just a total lack of effort on their part, Clara. Worse than this boy."

Shortly afterwards, Father turned to other suppliers with more reliable credentials. So the Royal Air Force was able to make good use of his donations.

Father's reward was a tiny Royal Air Force badge to be worn in the buttonhole. As with all his other insignia - Masonic, Rotarian, Pharmaceutical, Sporting - Father kept the lot in a leather collar-box along with a mass of old coins.

Four years passed before hostilities ended. Only then - to anticipate things - did there take place Wrexham's Own Victory Parade. After passing along High Street the military joined the leading townsfolk gathered together in St. Giles's Parish Church. From the pew at the front, Major Hurford-Jenkins glanced in our direction. His bloodshot eye was fixed upon Father's lapel. To the surprise of the rest of us, Father was seen to be sporting his R.A.F. insignia for the occasion.

"Didn't know you were a flying hero, Knox Mawer" chortled Major H.J.

"The war may be over, Jenkins," said Father "but there are some Secret Missions that have to remain that way."

The organ crashed into the National Anthem. Once again, Father had delivered a knockout blow with one of his unforgettable exit lines.

CHAPTER FIVE

HANDS ACROSS THE SEA

"Off at last, Clara" exclaimed Father "a merciful release!"

"Isn't that rather hard on the boy, George?" Mother ventured. She naturally assumed that Father was referring to my pending departure from home into the army.

"I'm talking about those yankee soldiers, for heaven's sake."

My narrative has returned to the phase of the War when, as with so many parts of the country, contingencies of General Eisenhower's force became a familiar sight in the Wrexham neighbourhood. This caused a dangerous rise in Father's blood pressure.

"The petrol attendant at Clark's Garage told me that the last convoy left in the Shrewsbury direction first thing this morning. I'd begun to think they'd never go."

"Well they are our allies, dear" said Mother "and you did get on very well with Mr. Schneider in the end."

"Noisy immoral barbarians for the most part!" Father persisted. "Why Dr.Brock was telling me only the other day that in his practice alone he's got twelve unmarried expectancies on his hands. I blame it on the Park of course."

"The park, George?"

He was referring to the Bradley Road Recreation Ground. Most pedestrians could not see over its hedge. But because of his immense height, Father, unfortunately, could.

"My letter to the mayor about the disgraceful goings-on in there did no good, Clara. However, I was able to loan my hockey-referee's whistle to the park keeper."

Alas, Father's instructions to Evan Price, the park-keeper, seem to have been a little vague.

"When exactly am I supposed to blow the whistle?" had been Evan's reaction.

The Schneider saga, however, had begun when I was next home on leave from artillery training.

"The housing officer has been on to me, Clara" Father announced. "Apparently, we're to have one of these damned yankee officers actually billeted upon us. Entirely against my will."

There could hardly have been a politer representative of his country than Lieutenant Arnold P. Schneider of the 244th Infantry. The lieutenant accepted without demur the icy discomfort of Father's attic. Nor did he complain when he was allowed merely the use of the back staircase.

"Occupied Territory, Clara," Father announced "That sums up our intolerable situation."

"But we hardly know he's here George" said Mother "he comes in so quietly in the evening and he's gone before breakfast time."

Father was unmoved.

No doubt non-fraternisation would have continued indefinitely save for an unexpected development.

Father had just converted our suburban garden into a farm - "part of my war effort, Clara."   Up at first light to make a tour of inspection, he encountered Mr. Schneider as he was leaving through the rear gates.

"That's a mighty fine hog you're raisin' there sir" I heard the lieutenant say, through the open window of my bedroom. Father was exceedingly proud of the pig for which he had a special shed erected behind the duck pond, adding yet another complaint from our neighbours.

"Could you maybe use some leftovers from our cookhouse sir?"

"That's exceedingly kind of you" said Father gruffly.

Within a couple of hours, the lieutenant returned with a jeep load of offerings. When this was repeated for the whole of the week, even Father was obliged to revise his verdict upon Lieutenant Schneider.

"I've invited him to Sunday Lunch, Clara" he said.

The greatest surprise however, was when Lieutenant Schneider buttonholed Father in Grosvenor Road with the enquiry "May I have the honour, sir, of accompanying you to your Place of Worship, next Sabbath?"

"I can see no objection" Father said "Parish church, 10.45 a.m."

"Leave the transport to me" Father was told.

The sight of Father. in his trilby hat and dark grey Sunday suit, being driven in the front passenger seat of Lieutenant Schneider's open jeep to the St. Giles' Parish Church quickly became the talk of the town.

Mr. Arthur Camp, the organist, caught sight of the stars and stripes flying over the bonnet as he was turning into the church gates.

"For goodness sake Canon Davies" he expostulated to the vicar "Why didn't you tell me that Mr. Roosevelt was coming?"

"Mr. Roosevelt?"

It was well known that Mr. Camp watched too many newsreels at the Odeon Cinema and had developed obsessive delusions about the War-Leader. He was also extremely short-sighted.

"There's no organ music in Hymns Ancient and Modern for the American National Anthem neither!"

Perhaps there was a fleeting resemblance sufficient to confuse the old organist between Father in his all-weather motoring cloak and the U.S. President. Disenchantment quickly set in though, when the figure behind the American Flag was recognised as G.R. Knox Mawer.

With the morning service over, the Anglo-American duo returned to Resthaven for lunch.

"That sure was a tasty blueberry pie" enthused Lieutenant Schneider to Mother. "Blackberries" corrected Father "picked by my daughter Rosemary. One of her Sunday tasks."

Rosemary, looking as crushed as the blackberries, hurried to refill the visitors glass with Father's ginger beer.

"Tell me Colonel" said Father expansively - since the only army officer he knew was Worshipful Brother Colonel Jarvis Roberts, he seemed to assume all officers were colonels. "Tell me colonel. What is our function, now that the rest of your troops have left the area?"

"Well Sir I'm attached to the Royal Welsh Fusiliers headquarters in High Town. Guess my business is Communication."

"Fornication?!" said Father turning purple. He had forgotten to remove one of his Air Raid Ear Plugs, a familiar omission. The Lieutenant hastily raised his voice.

"I'm organising some morale boosting broadcasts from the BBC Light Programme."   Father was impressed despite himself.

It was at a later date when I was home on another army pass that I found that Trans Atlantic relations at Resthaven had become so warm that "Ed" our military guest was invited by Father to chair the "festive board" every evening. Not that it was particularly festive, except where Ed supplemented the cold beetroot and spam with GI fare. Needless to say Father drew the line over the distribution of chewing gum.

"It is true that Mr. Schneider will be providing entertainment for the Masonic Ladies Evening George?" Mother enquired.

Father nodded.

"Guess I can't get Major Glen Miller and the band of the Allied Expeditionary Forces up to Wrexham town" said our guest "so I'm doing the next best thing with an armful of his discs. Ronnie'll be with us of course?"   I was about to excuse myself, as a non mason, when Father interrupted.

"Yes. The boy had better come along and make himself useful."

The Masonic Hall was crowded for the occasion.

"No thank you, Brother Hayes" Father said "we shall not need your violin performance of The Lost Chord this year."   Mrs Bagnall Bury's piano offering "The Blue Danube" was also declined.

"Won't you be wanting my wife and I to sing our usual selections from the Merry Widow, Worshipful Brother Knox Mawer?" asked the assistant director of ceremonies, Worshipful Brother Sydney Hughes, the stout energetic High Street draper.

"Not this year" he was sternly told.

From my seat at the back, I watched with bated breath as Lieutenant Schneider tried to explain the workings of the US Field Juke Box, a machine set up behind Father's table. It was typical of Father that, although somewhat out of his depth, he was determined to remain in charge.

"Would you mind, sir, announcing the first item?" asked Lieutenant Schneider.

"Certainly" replied Father. "What is it?"

"It's Dinah Shore singing 'Is you or is you ain't my baby'"

"Baby?!" frowned Father, still brooding over the number of unwanted pregnancies in Wrexham.

Mr. Schneider tried again.

"Well how about Fats Waller, with 'Your feet's too big'."

"Who is Mr. Waller?" asked Father. He tried what he believed Americans called a wisecrack. "Is he some kind of chiropodist?!"

The Lieutenant smiled indulgently. "He's a great jazz pianist."

By this time the audience were getting restive.

"Right. Let's get them 'in the mood' anyway" said Lieutenant Schneider, putting on the record of that title.

By the time the Glenn Miller Orchestra had played half of IN THE MOOD, I saw Father inserting both of his Air Raid Earplugs. He stood up to thank Lieutenant Schneider and to substitute Brother Hayes' Lost Chord on the violin. Little did he know that 'In the Mood' is famous for it's numerous false endings and so each time the music seemed to come to a halt Father rose up only to be blasted down again by the screaming trumpet section of the band.

"Well thank you, Lieutenant Schneider" he gasped finally. "We shall now revert to our usual musical fare."

"No! No!" insisted several voices, already well In The Mood. "Let's have more swing!"

Brother Walter Jackson bent down in Father's direction to explain.

"Some of the younger masons and their wives want the records to continue. After all, we of the older generation have to give way upon this sort of occasion."

Still protesting, Father was persuaded to sit down and I was summoned to sit by him. Behind his rigid head, the juke box started up again.

"In a little honky-tonky village in Texas" sang the Pied Pipers. "There's a man who plays the best piano by far..."

Mrs Bagnall Bury, in the arms of a rhythm-crazed brother Llewellyn Morris, whirled past Father's table, knocking over his ginger beer and glass.

"He can play piano any way'at you like it..."   Even the Worshipful Master was tapping his feet.

"Beat me Daddy eight to the bar" sang the vocal group to the final boogie woogie crescendo.

Father caught sight of me on the row behind. "What on earth is that boy grinning about, Clara?" I heard him demand, above the merriment.

Lieutenant Schneider was on his feet again. "Here's a toast to the best daddy of them all. He's certainly been like a daddy to me."

There was a sound of applause. Father blew his nose forcefully, rather pink in the face, before making a rapid exit. But on the way home in the car he was distinctly heard to whistle under his breath, the Beat Me Daddy tune. And as he trod the stairs to bed I noticed him rap out some kind of primitive rhythm on the bannisters. The words "Honky Tonky Village in Texas" faded behind his bedroom door.

Had Father become infected with the boogie-woogie craze I wondered?

However, a few weeks later, a parcel arrived from Lieutenant Schneider - now in London - with a complimentary slip. The famous record it contained was placed, upon Father's direction, in the loft - there to gather an infinite layer of dust.

CHAPTER SIX

NATIONAL DISSERVICE

Invariably Father's more alarming pronouncements upon my fate came at the breakfast table. This one had occurred on June 14th 1943. The war was then in its fourth year and I was aged seventeen.

"Gibbon says he'll actually take on this boy, Clara" Father suddenly announced to Mother. "Much to my surprise I may add."

Up to that moment the usual silence had been maintained at the table. The BBC news of the world conflict had been absorbed and switched off. Only Father's routine bout of hiccups disturbed the uneasy calm. Not that any of us four children or Mother ever dared to notice this extraordinary performance. His practice of draining his morning glass of ginger beer at one gulp always caused his digestive system to revolt.

There was no chance of revolt from any other quarter. Father's awesome presence dominated the family, his High Street chemist-shop and the local Masonic Order.

"Did you say Gibbon dear?" Mother inquired gently.

"Colonel Gibbon, for heaven's sake. My fellow Standard Bearer at Grand Lodge."

Mother nodded with a calm smile, although this was the first time any of us had ever heard the name.

"The Colonel runs a course for young artillerymen on Salisbury Plain" Father continued. "Takes only 17 year old volunteers of course." He glanced sharply in my direction.

"I've arranged for the boy to be down at Wrexham Recruiting Office at nine sharp, tomorrow morning."

It was no surprise to discover that everything relating to my enlistment, next day, was entirely cut and dried.

"Your Father did warn us about your hopelessly unmilitary posture" was the only remark addressed to me by the officer in charge, but I have assured him that that will be speedily put right on the Larkhill Parade Ground."

From here on I was Army number 14438573, or 573 for short. Fortunately the icy nissen hut in which I found myself accommodated on Salisbury Plain was not too great a shock. After all, up until then I had lived in Wrexham and worse still under Father's roof, amid acres of bare linoleum, where the family slept on iron bedsteads with the alarm clocks permanently set at six a.m. It was not so different to be roused by the buglers of Larkhill Gunnery School.

Upon the wooden bunk underneath mine slept Gunner Horsley, an ex-Borstal Inmate for whom letter writing was not a natural talent. However I managed to ingratiate myself with him by helping out with pen and paper. His lady friend in Hackney was impressed by the love letters ghosted by me.

"What's this ere?" demanded Regimental Sergeant Major 'Tiger' Gogerty, inspecting our beds one morning. He was referring to a rough draft of the next missive to Enid Bagley of 15, Crimea

Terrace, London East 14. Tiger's red rimmed eyes had fallen on the opening lines 'Shall I compare thee to a summers day. Thou art more lovely and more temperate.'   Enid might have been impressed by the Bard - but *not* R.S.M. Gogerty, whose dislocated nose and battered face suggested a preference for the boxing ring rather than literature. Under pressure, Horsley betrayed me as the letter writer.

"Fall in the educated f ---- g idiot" was thereafter the familiar summons to me whether for square bashing on the parade grounds, or at gun drill on the artillery range.

By now the allied armies had landed in France. Such chances as I might have had of getting into Tiger's good books were quickly dashed when I went down with mumps the day before the regiment sailed for Normandy. "Bloody typical" was Tiger's comment as I was carried past on my way to the isolation ward of the Folkestone Maternity Hospital. Apparently it was the only quarantine accommodation that could be found, and because of complications, I was incarcerated there for several months.

By the time I caught up with the regiment at a base camp 28 miles north of Antwerp, military operations were drawing to a close.

"Jerry may not be quite finished" roared Tiger Gogerty as my battery stood to attention in front of him.

"Reckon he might be trying to fire off his secret weapons from the Hook of Holland". He singled out Lance Bombadier Taffy Narbeth for attention.

"Take 573 with you in a 15 cwt truck" he decreed "and do a spot of reconnaissance."

Taffy was well known to the rest of us as a connoisseur of 'The Good Life'. Until that moment he had managed to spend most of his overseas service in the Montgomery Leave Centre in Brussels on the pretext that he was "rounding up deserters." Considerably overweight, and with long blonde hair carefully combed under his beret, Taffy had no intention of running into danger at this late stage of the war. He drove us a certain distance into the Netherlands and upon discovering that the dykes had burst and we were becoming water-logged, he decided that his first priority was to "protect them spark plugs (of our army truck) from getting rotten damp. Take the binoculars, with some iron rations, and do your best, mate," he instructed "I'll run her to the nearest Service Corps Station for maintenance."

I made my way across a turnip field where I encountered a farmer who knew no English. He was of a surly disposition but by means of sign language and a large carton of American cigarettes - a luxury of immense value in March 1945 - I persuaded him to allow me to billet myself in a disused windmill.

I spent the next week or two constructing an observation post at the top of the building before setting myself the task of keeping a nervous lookout for hostile rockets. Unfortunately there was something wrong with my RT equipment and I seemed to have lost contact with the outside world. At least no one responded to my regular communiqués. After maybe two or three weeks in the windmill I sighted Taffy roaring up again in the truck.

"What the hell d'you think you're doing Knoxy?" he called.

"I should have thought it was obvious" I responded with what dignity I could muster "I'm endeavouring to carry out a reconnaissance on the Hook of Holland as ordered."

"You must be the only man in the whole bloody army who doesn't know that the war's over!" he said.

He pushed aside his victory trophies, a German helmet and a swastika flag, to make room for me alongside him.

"We're all posted back to the U.K. to get ready for the Far Eastern lark" he explained as we set off back to the base camp.

After an appallingly rough voyage across the channel from Ostend, we landed at Folkestone where it was raining.

"You lot" announced Tiger Gogerty "is the first unit back from the British Liberation Army. So throw back your bleedin' shoulders and set your bayonets in your rifles. Remember the proud slogan of the RA which is 'Right of the line'!"

Our march through the main street to the railway was not exactly a rousing moment in history. Victory Parades had already become a thing of the past. Queues of resentful shoppers lined up outside empty shop windows took absolutely no notice of us whatsoever.

Back on Salisbury Plain, during June and July 1945, Tiger Gogerty made only a single call upon my services. It was one which he lived to regret.

"Afraid 573 is the only man available for you, sir," he reported to Captain D'Arcy.

I managed to start up the Humber Snipe staff car, as the Captain settled into the front passenger seat.

"Make for Stonehenge" he commanded.

"Amazing construction sir" I said, as the ancient circle came into view, through the early morning mist, "Archaeologists date it back to 4000 BC they say". As I peered out for a closer inspection I felt a violent lurch as the near side wheel disappeared into what must have been some kind of slit trench. It took an hour or more to retrieve the situation, but with a bit of help from members of the Pioneer Corps, armed with picks and shovels, the vehicle was safely righted.

"Put this man on a charge, Sergeant Major" snapped Captain D'Arcy upon our return.

Fortunately the RSM's investigation into my driving misdemeanour was interrupted by the superior orders for the regiment to proceed to the Far Eastern theatre of war, and I was dispatched upon embarkation leave. However, just as I was beginning the journey home to Father, the Japanese gave up. Or as Captain D'Arcy put it "The Nips have thrown in the towel."

Perhaps in my own long-running war where Father was concerned the time had come for me to do the same thing.

CHAPTER SEVEN

BLUEBIRDS OVER RESTHAVEN

The last thing I want so suggest is that Father did not share the general relief that the war had ended. But when, on August 12th 1945, I arrived at the GWR Wrexham General for leave, he was angrily consulting his pocket watch.

"Ten minutes late" he barked. Fortunately, on this occasion, Father was referring to the train, not to me. Even so, it was evident that things at home were unchanged. The only sign of relaxation in the iron regime was that my list of Father's "Holiday tasks" on the sideboard omitted the dreaded "muck out pig shed". The pig had apparently met its end in my absence. Not that there was any pork for supper that evening. Just the usual "cold collation" of spam and beetroot. In the background, from our three tiered gothic wireless set Vera Lynn was trilling " Bluebirds over.....white cliffs of Dover....there'll be love and laughter....peace ever after."

From Father, however, there was the customary silence, punctuated by an occasional hiccup, as he downed his Stone's Ginger Beer.

"They've clearly no further use for this boy, Clara. Particularly as his sole contribution to the war in Europe seems to have been getting himself lost."

"Well they definitely want me to report back" I said. "Have to check in with Battery H.Q. now at Woolwich Arsenal to await further orders."

A look of extreme irritation passed over Father's face. He obviously had other plans in mind. With a sweeping gesture, he took out from his breast pocket the Black Swan Fountain Pen. A few minutes later, he handed me a letter, addressed to my Commanding Officer.

"Sir" it read "with regard to 14438573 KNOX MAWER R. still under your command. Surely there is something constructive that he and his colleagues can do back in our own country, while still in uniform. As President of the Pharmaceutical Society, I have a serious problem with a large bomb-crater outside our premises in Bloomsbury Square. Even my son, 573, should be of some assistance in a labour-force to fill in this danger-trap and eyesore. I have other suggestions for USEFUL WORK AT HOME. Now that the Hun and the Nip have been put to rout, one enemy remains- that of idleness in the young. I await your response."

He received no reply. Colonel Gibbon did not refer to the matter, except to inquire kindly if my father was under any form of medication.

"No sir," I said "apart from a stock of eucalyptus lozenges he always carries in his waistcoat pocket."

The C.O. paused reflectively.

"Still, perhaps sending you on compassionate leave might help, if only for your mother's sake."

One such period of leave followed another. "What on earth's going on Clara" Father demanded each time, "is that boy coming or going?!"

Arriving home the week before Christmas, I tried to enter Resthaven as unobtrusively as possible. I dropped my kit-bag in the darkness of the back passage, the plan being to creep up the stairs with a couple of bottles of ale. How was I to know that this was Father's storage-area for fifty Civil Defence Helmets, "snapped up" as one of his 'bargains.'

The avalanche of crashing metal around me was deafening. There came an indignant snort from the sitting room, as Father appeared in the doorway, anxiously followed by Mother.

"Well that's the first job he's got himself tomorrow morning, Clara" he said "every helmet to be numbered and stacked on my greenhouse shelves for the seedlings."

There was a heavy fall of snow that night, which slowed down my work removing the helmets, and it was dusk before I could make a swift getaway. I had arranged to meet up with an old school-chum, Gordon Hughes, whose flat feet had enabled him to avoid the call-up. By the time we left the Golden Lion that evening, Gordon was tipsy. His boisterous carols reached a particularly noisy level as we came alongside Number 26 Grosvenor Road.

"Good King Wenceleslas looked out, on the Feast of Stephen," sang Gordon full blast.

Dramatically, at the same moment, the curtains of the main bedroom parted to disclose a distinctly Regal Figure in a voluminous maroon dressing gown.

Evidently Father was undressing after an evening of masonic ritual, his royal insignia of office glinting in the moonlight. Even Gordon was unnerved by the vision.

"Yonder peasant, who is he?" he quavered, his voice fading a little "Where and what his dwelling?"

"I know perfectly well who you are and where and what your dwelling, Gordon Hughes!" Father's thunderous voice shattered a large icicle suspended from the guttering. "I shall be round to complain to your parents first thing tomorrow."

On the morrow however, luckily for Gordon, Father's attention was directed elsewhere. The focus of his indignation was the large holly tree, which stood at the far end of the hedge that divided Father's garden from that of his old adversary, Major Hurford Jenkins, of Number 28. At Mother's suggestion I was dispatched with a pair of clippers, to bring in some branches for decoration. "A spot of colour" was how she put it. It was always an effort to brighten the grim interior of Resthaven.

Returning to the table I braced myself to deliver the bad news.

"I'm afraid Major Hurford-Jenkins has stolen a march on us, Father."

Violently he pushed away the remains of his two duck eggs.

"What on earth do you mean?"

"The major has been out there already. and stripped the tree. Not a single berry left, I'm afraid."

Father's neck above his stiff size-18 wing collar was now of a shade to match the brightest of holly berries. He drew a deep breath as he prepared to launch his counter-offensive.

"Very well then. Jenkins has cut off my holly. I shall cut off his water supply!"

The stop cock in the party-wall which controlled the joint supply was a permanent source of friction.

"You can tell Jenkins it's to prevent a freeze-up."

Unfortunately for Father's plan, the freeze-up had already taken place, and it was impossible to turn the mechanism in any direction. "Easily fixed," Father said. Far from fixing things his manic use of the coal-hammer gave a day's work to Ashley's, the Wrexham plumbers.

"Wonder's never cease!" Father exclaimed. He had moved across to the morning table to sort out the mail. "Here's something from Hurford Jenkins!"

On the back of a large envelope I caught sight of the impression of a purple coloured rubber-stamp. Slightly smudged it read - FROM MAJOR A. HURFORD JENKINS, ARMY DENTAL CORPS. RETIRED.

"Perhaps the fellow's decided to contribute towards the plumbers bill."

Mother and I watched with bated breath as Father opened the missive. At the same moment, there was a large popping sound. What looked like a Christmas cracker erupted into Father's lap, followed by a shower of streamers and a toy whistle.

Father pushed back his chair, quivering with rage.

"This is the last straw!"

The Major's slapstick sense of humour was notorious. No doubt his misguided intention was to restore goodwill for the festive season. Father's reaction was an immediate consignment of the offending package to the open fireplace. Without another word, he marched off into his study.

What would come next, I wondered. Open warfare?   Or at least a personal confrontation with the enemy. There must be some sort of release for Father's pent-up rage.

But it seemed he was 'building up his Case for Prosecution.'
Just by chance, I came across a large jotter on his desk. Under the heading 'JENKINS' was a list of the Major's misdeeds - "unlawful spread of pesticide, inadequate drainage, leaking of foul air from surgery-fan" and so on. Father had now added the words "delivery of explosive substance, contrary to postal regulations."

That very day, he was provided with yet another item of complaint. While he was outside, checking the amount of coke I had shovelled into the boiler to warm his growing frames, the Major's two grandsons were playing in the snow. One of them had sneaked up behind the wash-house and sent Father's homburg flying across into their garden with a snowball.

"Well aimed!" we heard Major H.J. chortle as he was clearing his drive. "Better than a hand-grenade!"

The boy had beat a hasty retreat but Father stood still. "Can't imagine you handling any grenades in the Army Dental Corps" he called over. "Can't even take aim with a dentist's drill from what I've heard."

With that Father turned on his heel and returned indoors. He subsequently sent me to recover the homburg, although I had to pretend that I could not find it. I did not dare describe to him the snowman now erected by the Jenkins' French window, bearing Father's distinctly ample proportions and wearing his missing hat together with a pair of steel spectacles.

This was the point when luckily some Good News arrived to bring a welcome distraction.

There was a shrill ring on our doorbell and a telegram handed in for me. My Battery was now to be used for garrison duty in India, the train connection for Southampton must be caught at Crewe on the afternoon of January 1st.

The morning of my departure coincided with a rather noisy cocktail-party, thrown by the Hurford-Jenkins' which meant a further rise in Father's blood pressure.

"Austerity is what Sir Stafford Cripps the Chancellor of the Exchequer has called for, Clara!   Not downright extravagance of that sort!"

He retreated to his study in a black mood. I noticed he was armed with the familiar black tome with which he always rehearsed his lines for the next Masonic Lodge, a ritual designed to induce comparative calm and concentration. All in vain. Just moments later there was a loud screeching of brakes. A quick glance through the conservatory window told me that Hurford Jenkins, with the assistance no doubt of several large gins, had been rapidly backing his car out of Grosvenor Road when the front wheels skidded on a patch of ice in the gutter.

"Now what's that fool of a man up to?!" demanded Father, hurrying to the front door.

No sooner had he spoken when the Major's vehicle spun round in a circle and collided into our gatepost with a sickening crunch.

"Obviously a case of drunken driving!" Father bellowed at the Major through the windscreen. "Totally reckless behaviour!"

"Entirely the fault of the elements" explained Mr. Hurford Jenkins. He was struggling to open the car-door which had jammed into the gate.

"Elements be damned!"

I picked up my kitbag,. It was time for me to go. I made my farewells to Mother. "You may still be in the army, but at least you're going off into a world at peace" she said.

"Not as far as I'm concerned" snapped Father.

Back in the hallway, he had grabbed the telephone to summon Inspector Jones, a masonic colleague, at the Regent Street Police Station. To avoid the scene at the front of the house I took the rear exit.

"Goodbye Father. Happy New Year" I called. Holding out the receiver, he had paused to take breath.

"And there's also a charge of stolen property, a holly bush and a brand new homburg hat," the diatribe continued. "Not to mention the dispatch of dangerous material by post....."

I closed the door behind me. The world at large was still celebrating the onset of peace, but for Father, the Cold War had well and truly begun.

CHAPTER EIGHT

ISLANDS OF HOPE AND GLORY

For once, luck seemed to be on my side. After demobilisation, an army grant enabled me to become a qualified barrister, with a Cambridge Law Degree. I also landed a job in H.M. Overseas Judiciary, far away from the Cold War- Father's or anybody else's, In fact my posting was so far away that nobody knew where it was.

But that was looking six months ahead. First I had to be vetted by the Whitehall official who held this particular key to my future.

"We've decided to accept you on probation, as a Relieving Magistrate, in the Western Pacific High Commission Territories" said the Head of Establishments at the Colonial Office.

I nodded eagerly.

"You'll be answerable, of course, to Chief Justice Sir Neville Gawsby himself. So I'd advise you to familiarise yourself with Sir Neville's many publications on law and native custom in that part of the world."

"Where do I do that sir?"

"In our library on the ground floor of course."

Within a door marked READING ROOM, I was welcomed by Mr. Crowther, the librarian. He led me across to a revolving globe in the bay window. There he spanned a large blue segment of the Pacific with his bony hand.

"You'll have a judicial parish of millions of square miles, my friend" he observed.

"Yes indeed" I said.

"Your parishioners being almost entirely fish" he added, stifling a wheezing laugh into his handkerchief.

The globe creaked to a noisy standstill. Two elderly memsahibs, at work on biographies of their late husbands, turned from their labours with critical looks in my direction. "Is the notice for NO TALKING totally ignored these days?!" one of them remarked.

"Better follow me into the basement" whispered Mr. Crowther, stealing out behind them.

"You'll find Sir Neville's books on the very top shelf there" he pointed out before leaving me to my own resources.

Unfortunately the angle of the book-ladder involved a steep climb. Just as I was reaching out for Sir Neville's CORONER'S GUIDE TO THE SAVAGE ISLES, I missed my footing and received a sharp crack on the temple from his massive tome, JURY TRIAL AMONG THE HEAD-HUNTERS OF NEW GUINEA.

"Are you alright?" enquired Mr. Crowther, shaking me back to full consciousness.

Despite my protest, he insisted on calling for help. As the stretcher-bearers carried me off to the Medical Centre, he pressed a paperback into my hand. PROBLEMS OF EQUITY IN SABU SABU BY SIR NEVILLE GAWSBY was the title.

"I hope I'm not troubling you unnecessarily" I said to the elderly nurse in charge of first aid.

"I hope so too," she snapped, "when I was matron at the Livingstone Hospital in Uganda, I should have given short shrift to a colonial service officer who bothered me with a minor abrasion of this sort."

She looked me up and down critically. "They're not thinking of sending *you* out to the tropics, are they?"

"Well as a matter of fact they are" I said.

"Well you don't look particularly robust to me" she said. "So make sure you have the whole range of injections at the School of Tropical Medicine."

I took her advice before reporting back to Mr. Langford Smith for the final details of my assignment.

"Sir Neville wants you to go directly to Vunaki Somo. You'll be sent further details in the post."

I was about to ask about leave conditions when Mr. L.S. interrupted me.

"Any particular reason for giving me the Nazi Salute, Knox Mawer?"

"It's the cholera vaccination, sir" I explained "my right arm's gone so stiff that it just has to be held up."

With an unsympathetic nod, he brought the interview to an end.

My letter of appointment indicated that I should make my own arrangements for the outward passage.

"Could I have that name again" said the booking clerk at the Wrexham Travel Agency. I spelt it out for him. He was not getting much help from his railway map of North Wales. After pouring over the World Atlas with a magnifying glass, he at last discovered a few dots just west of the Cook Islands.

"Transport's going to be your problem."

I managed to solve this by flying QUANTAS to Samoa, and from there, the missionary ship JOHN WESLEY provided me with a cabin to my destination.

The local Minister, a grim-faced New Zealand Baptist, was disembarking with me.

"Well brother" he observed as we sped towards the jetty in a small landing-boat "you'll find the last Magistrate, Rob Garfield, a hard act to follow. A fine man, was Rob Garfield, and a devout Christian."

Apparently, it had been my predecessor's habit to attend the Sunday Morning Prayer Meeting. I was willing to put in an appearance myself, in the front pew, but the Minister's prayers droned on endlessly.

Eventually the coconut matting was too much for my bare
knees, and I crept out between the rows of devout islanders, to
take a breather under the banana trees. Afterwards, I managed to
have a word with the Minister, as he squeezed behind the wheel
of his baby Austin.

"I'm sorry padre" I said "I'll bring my own cushion next
time!"

His large, lugubrious features glared up at me with distaste.
Alongside him on the front passenger seat was his doleful
bloodhound, so similar in appearance to his master that it was
difficult to distinguish man from dog.

"Not a patch on Rob Garfield" I heard one of them murmur as
they shot away in a cloud of dust.

CHAPTER NINE

WALTZING MATILDA

As it turned out, my stay in Vunaki Somo was cut short by a cable from Chief Justice Sir Neville Gawsby. "Imperative that you complete outstanding cases forthwith, before checking in at H.Q."

Fortunately, I had already disposed of the indictable Pineapple Fraud, involving Tomsi Bilevu, treasurer of the island agriculture trust fund. A gifted musician, he was now performing a lengthy spell of Community Service with the massed banjos of the prison band.

This only left the trial of the village witch doctor, for casting a spell of infertility over the wife of Chief Napoleoni. I had wisely deferred this hearing until the end of the Cause List, by which time the prosecution withdrew the charge because the lady in question had given birth to twins.

With work on the island completed, my next step was to report to Suba, capital of British Oceania, for my interview with Sir Neville.

An enterprising Australian, Ashley Patterson, operated a small seaplane service for charter flights. He agreed to take me and welcomed me onto the aircraft with the words "Park your bum, sport." By this he clearly meant the empty co-pilot's seat up front. Despite his bluff manner, Captain Patterson was a brilliant aviator and within a couple of hours, he landed me safely in Suba Bay.

Sir Neville's well appointed chambers commanded a splendid view of the bay. The air conditioning system was purring gently as he greeted me: "Come in, come in."

Sleek and well fed, Sir Neville wore an immaculately creased light grey cotton suit. On a side table stood a silver coffee pot and cups, along with a large plate of chocolate biscuits.

"Help yourself dear chap" he said. I drank my coffee but declined a second biscuit.

"I do wish you'd finish off the plate" said the Chief Justice. "If you don't mind my saying so, you must be the skinniest officer in the service."

"I'm perfectly fit though sir" I replied.

"That's good to hear, because although you'll be based here, you'll be more or less continuously out on circuit in the more distant dependencies."

Sir Neville stood up and strode across to a desk in the bay window.

"However your first assignment is explained in these papers."

I peered over Sir Neville's shoulder at an important-looking document headed Ravuma Mineral Rights. FOR IMMEDIATE ACTION.

"Valuable phosphate deposits have been discovered on that particular atoll" Sir Neville explained. "So it is essential that a Land Court is held forthwith, to sort out who owns what."

He handed me the folder. "Brief yourself on the situation and please embark upon the assignment as speedily as possible."

I thought I had done pretty well to persuade the Samoan Skipper of an inter-island copra schooner to make a detour to land me on the atoll in question. Back in the Chief Justice's department I had been told that all the necessary arrangements were in hand.

"Where on earth is everybody?" I asked myself, scanning the landing pier for some sort of human activity. Suddenly I heard my name roared out by a very English voice. From within the door of a banana warehouse there stepped an immensely tall figure, craggy and grizzled, in rolled up khaki shorts and a soiled sun-helmet.

"J.S. Pennington's the name" he said, giving my hand a painful crunch. "I'm the District Commissioner for Bai Lalevu and this territory comes within my patch."

"How do you travel about your domain?" I asked.

"I've an official motor-yacht. It's anchored off the north shore. I've already send a message on my radio transmitter to Sir Neville. I've told him that when you've wound up your legal work here, I'll take you back to the mainland."

Suddenly he dug into the pocket of his bush jacket and produced a bosun's whistle. With two loud blasts, he summoned a cheerful member of the crew and directed him to help me across with my baggage to the Rest House.

"I'll join you there for a sundowner" he promised.

The Rest house, a ramshackle bungalow overlooking the lagoon, had been stocked with provisions for my stay. The sun had gone down and a cool breeze had sprung up by the time J.S. had arrived, with two bottles of whiskey under his arm.

"Now what do you know about these islanders?" he began, pouring out two enormous glassfuls of whiskey before settling back into one of the deckchairs on the front verandah.

"Well I propose to assess all claims to mineral rights upon equitable principles."

J.S. downed his drink and quickly poured another. "I hope Sir Neville made sure that you brought a judge's wig."

I nodded.

"If you prefer gin" said J.S. "there's half a dozen bottles of Gordon's in my locker, so just say the word."

"Afraid I've no head for alcohol" I explained.

"And also on a diet with your food from what I can see" said J.S. gloomily. He stroked his beaky nose in contemplation. "Damned good thing that you brought the wig. At least that will help to give you a spot of authority."

"I don't quite see" I began.

"Without the full-bottomed regalia, old boy, you wouldn't have a snowball's chance in hell of gaining their respect here."

"I hope I can hold a judicial enquiry as well as the next man" I protested indignantly.

J.S. shook his head.

"Not without the wig, I'm afraid. You see, authority is measured in size here. Size and weight. It's as simple as that. Unfortunately you fail in both departments."

J.S. lit up a cheroot, shook out the last drop from the first bottle of whiskey and opened the second.

"I can promise you one thing, J.S." I said. "Although I don't tip the scales like a heavyweight boxer, I'll try to make up for it with the old brain work."

J.S. stood up to his full height and drew over his shoulders a tattered hide shawl. "I've arranged for you to sit in the tribal meeting hall tomorrow, and I've impressed upon the locals that you'll be wearing 'magic hair'. That's gone down very well. With a bit of luck, you'll be regarded as an Oracle."

He clamped a friendly arm on my shoulder as he took his leave. "Don't worry, Sunny Jim" he said. "I gathered from what Sir Neville told me that you would be judicially arrayed on top."
He tapped the side of his temple, took one last swig of the whiskey bottle and disappeared into the night.

For myself, I should have managed alright, had it not been that the Rest House bedroom overlooked the Mangrove-Swamp. The consequences were disastrous. Tormented by mosquitoes and with land-crabs nibbling at the soles of my feet, it was almost dawn before I fell into an exhausted sleep. Even so, I was determined next morning not to let the side down.

After a nutritious breakfast of paw-paw and coconut milk, I dressed in full regalia and made my way over to the Thatched Meeting Hall.

"Good man" said J.S. meeting me at the entrance. "Glad you've chosen the long wig. Can't overstress how much that will add to your mana."

"Mana?"

"Polynesian word for 'power'" he explained.

The sun was already high, and I was feeling distinctly uncomfortable.

"Hope you approve of the Seat of Justice, so to speak" said J.S. "I've had the crew at work on your behalf."

The Seat of Justice consisted of a kind of dais of bark-cloth, supported upon banana crates.

"There's been a lot of feeling on the island over rival claims to this new source of wealth," J.S. explained. "So I've decreed that nobody will be allowed at the proceedings as a precaution against trouble."

I was not at all keen upon a hearing "in camera". However, I deferred to J.S.'s long years of experience in this part of the world. He proved an excellent intermediary and interpreter, and with his assistance, I was able to hear evidence from all the leading families on the island and a considerable number of hangers-on.

"As you will have discovered" said J.S. "this is a matriarchal society. Property rights descend through the female line."

"Absolutely" I agreed. "So the royalties from phosphate exports will be distributed in accordance with that principle."

As my enquiry proceeded, it became clear that the leading matrons on the atoll were Chieftainess Matilda Bali along with five other women, each one of Amazonian proportions.

After a series of elaborate calculations I worked out a compromise scheme which would be fair to everybody. First of all, I had to obtain the assent of the Big Six.

"Would the following ladies, Matilda, Charlotti, Evelina, Martha, Saloti and Tota, kindly gather round me here on the bench so that we may discuss my proposal." This they did.

At first, I made no headway whatsoever.

"Don't you see, my good friends," I pleaded "if there is a limited surrender in respect of every individual claim, then the whole community will benefit."

Perhaps I was naive in my endeavour. And there was something else that I had failed to take into account. Why on earth had I not realised that J.S.'s platform was only made for my light frame. To invite alongside me what was, in effect, a ladies judo-team, was to court inevitable disaster. But I was still absorbed in my argument.

"Is there no giving way?" I repeated.

"There's giving way alright, laddy" called J.S. from the back of the court. He had arrived at a particularly crucial moment, just as the whole structure collapsed beneath me. I ended up with the gigantic Matilda sitting in my lap.

It was lucky that J.S. was there to give me assistance.

"Pop on your head-dress again" he said. "Meanwhile I'll have a pow-wow with the Big Six. Maybe they'll agree to my holding the phosphate funds as a Trustee."

Wiping an enormous bead of perspiration from my brow, I gave him the necessary go-ahead.

J.S. and the ladies conferred together under a nearby banyan tree. I must have dozed off because it was J.S. who shook me awake.

"Got them to agree to your proposed judgement" he announced. "In fact, they are so happy about the result, that I've invited the Big Six to a little farewell celebration on board the motor yacht."

Even my usual digestive troubles were forgotten that evening at J.S's party. Food and toddy-wine flowed in abundance.

"Care for a little music?" enquired J.S., fingering the keys of an ancient accordion. "What about the Blue Danube?"

Before I had time to move, Chieftainess Bali advanced upon me.

"Oh no!" I protested in vain.

"Perhaps you should have been warned" roared J.S. as she spun me around like an old sock caught in a spin drier. "On Ravuma, we call her Waltzing Matilda!"

CHAPTER TEN

TROUBLES IN PARADISE

After a lengthy tour of the Loloma Islands, I was feeling the wear and tear of some difficult forensic challenges. The great Raki Coconut Embezzlement Trial and the infamous Wytomba Monkey Fraud Case illustrate the kind of strain I had been under. There had been other crises too.

The counterfeiting activities of Bishop Roosevelt Mosesi, the notorious confidence-trickster from Funifatu had meant a call on the services of Interpol, greatly adding to my problems. A lengthy judicial enquiry in the appalling humidity of the Rainy Seasons followed. I was extremely jaded before it was possible to authorise a Government Exclusion Order against the wily evangelist.

Back to my home base at last, I was looking forward to a spot of relaxation after supper over my collection of British Empire stamps, when the telephone rang. Not without difficulty I picked up the receiver from where it had become entangled in the Samoan potted fern with which Noah, my bearer, liked to decorate my dining arrangements. I found myself assailed by the strident tones of Ursula Massingbird, Personal Assistant to my Head, Chief Justice Sir Neville Gawsby, and a formidable exponent of the overhead smash on the Vanua Levu Tennis Courts.

"I'm counting upon you for the Club Ball next week" she announced.

I would have tried some sort of excuse, but the risks were too great.

Everybody knew that she had the C.J. in the palm of her hand. For me not to fall in line with her plans would invite a disastrous Annual Report.

"What fun" I managed to reply, retrieving the Pitcairn Jubilee Issue from the remains of my mango pudding. "You can count on me, though dancing isn't my strong point."

The following Wednesday evening, I struggled into my dinner jacket - after dabbing a spot of Indian Ink over the usual signs of termite damage on the lapels   The Church Hall presented a lively scene, hung with palm leaves and the flags of all nations. For the first twenty minutes, Tupa Toranga and his South Sea Senenaders ('trusties' in everyday life, at the Island Penal Rehabilitation Centre) were playing their usual slow favourites, "Lovely Hula Hands and Hawaiian Love Song" and I was able to make my duty round of the senior ladies of the colony. When, however, at Ursula's request, the band was made to snap into rapid Viennese waltz-time, peril loomed. I could see Ursula sizing me up behind the steely glitter of her bifocals as she advanced upon me in her tartan taffeta ball-gown.
"Give it a whirl, Knoxy" she said. I was doing my best to comply. But on the third lap my foot caught in the flounce of her skirt, sending me reeling back in a solo spin of my own,   My collision with the lottery tub was sheer bad luck. It was just as the draw of the winning ticket was being made by Club President Chief Justice Gawsby himself. There was a titter from the surrounding dancers as a confetti-like shower of paper fluttered around his bald head.

"Are you trying to be funny?!" Ursula hissed under her breath. She helped Sir Neville compose himself for the Presidential Address.

"Fellow sportsfolk, one and all" began the C.J., with a vain effort to brush down his tails.

"I think I'll slip quietly away" I confided to Ursula. "Before I get into more trouble."

"Well don't forget about tomorrow morning's fixture", she warned "The Chief Justice intended to speak to you about it, after his speech."

Anxiously I asked for details. Regrettably most of her instructions were drowned in the grand finale, as the Serenaders embarked upon their version of the conga.

"And whatever you do" she concluded "make sure you're *on time.*"

It was just as I was making for the side exit that my arm was taken in an iron grip. It was none other than District Commissioner J.S. Pennington himself.

"Seems you're always in hot water, my boy" he said, lurching out of the bar, still shaking with laughter. "Time for me to take charge, eh?! We'll share a bicycle taxi. That's the only answer."

"But I'm going back to my bungalow" I said.

"So am I dear chap. You're putting me up for the night."

"In normal circumstances, J.S." I explained "you'd be most welcome. But the Public Works Department has not yet finished putting a new roof on the Guest Bedroom."

"Perfectly happy to share your sleeping quarters, old chap."

Common courtesy required me to give up the large charpoy and mosquito net to J.S. I found it difficult enough making myself comfortable on the hammock in the corner. Even so it was J.S's sensationally loud snore that proved beyond my endurance. I stole across the room and began to rummage in the medicine cupboard for my sleeping tablets. They were usually at the back of the medicaments on the first shelf - behind Shytes Prickly Heat Powder, and Dunby's Diarrhoea Mixture. In the light of my torch, I searched through the bottles of decongestants, the bronchial balsam, Coffin's Hip Balm and Mould's Expectorant. The search proved fruitless. Moving to the second shelf, I pushed aside Mump and Dunby's Rubbing Oil and Leecham's Glycerine, invaluable standbys of mine that had seen me through many a hot season. At that moment, I somehow knocked over two large flagons of Warts Liver Elixir.

"What the devil's going on, Knox-Mawer?" demanded J.S. aroused by the sudden clatter.

He switched on the light as my Breathe Easy Airball came rolling down onto my neck with a crash. It was followed by a cascade of Gross's Rapid Energy Release Powders.

"For heaven's sake, man!" exclaimed J.S. "The whole place is a bloody chemists shop. Talk about hypochondria!"

"I was only looking for my sleeping tablets" I ventured.

"Haven't I told you before, never to rely upon drugs" he admonished "especially in the tropics. A stiff drink is all you need. So perhaps you'd be good enough to fetch me a double, here and now."

I went out to the kitchen and after some delay in finding J.S.'s favourite brand, mixed him a large whiskey and soda.

Upon my return, a melancholy sight met my eyes. Every trace of a bottle, every pill had vanished and the medicine cupboard was totally bare.

"Got rid of all that rubbish for you" said J.S.

"But I...."

"Thrown the lot down the septic tank."

Surely not my Sleepwell Dorm Drops?" I complained, aghast.

"I don't know what those may be" he replied, downing the

contents of his glass and returning to his bed. "But if you follow my example, your problem's solved."

Closing his eyes, he resumed his noisy slumber.

I lay in despair. My wretched hammock had given way. After twisting sleepless for the next couple of hours, I went down to the beach hoping for a dawn swim.

There was no sign of J.S. Even my dip was not feasible, because without the protecting-net in position, I was not prepared to risk the sharks. J.S. had always said he was immune to the creatures. Apparently he had already had a swim and gone. When I returned to the house, I discovered he had left me a note.

"You'll thank me in the long run for getting rid of all those poisons. It could be a turning point in your career."   I felt not.

Hollow-eyed, I inspected my drawn features in the bathroom mirror. Once I'd shaved and breakfasted through I began to pull myself together. My mind however was almost a total blank. Except for the recollection that I was expected by the Chief Justice at any moment. Of the rest of Ursula Massingberd's briefing I could remember only the words - "Ten a.m. sharp. At the court."

"Strong coffee, maybe" I thought. "Should get the brain-cells moving."

Alas no. I glanced at my watch.

There were less than five minutes to go. A horrible dilemma had presented itself.

"At the Court" I repeated to myself "But WHICH ONE?"

Was I to sit with the Chief Justice on the Bench? - that tiresome case of Ratu Tuvalu's Master Forgery had been dragging on for two years. Or, since the C.J. was a keen tennis player, did he require me to make up a Mixed Four - with Ursula and the C.J's wife - on his private tennis court?   He sometimes liked to take an impromptu day off in the middle of the Sessions and I was often required to stand by.

I tried to telephone, but the line was dead, strangled overnight maybe by the predatory Samoan Fern.

After a few more seconds agonising upon the problem, the solution dawned.

Obvious.

The answer was a compromise. Tennis shorts and aertex vest under my judicial regalia.

"Your service, Knox-Mawer" called out the C.J., adjusting the net. Ursula was, of course, playing on his side. I was partnering the C.J's wife, a large lady with weak ankles.

It had indeed been simplicity itself to slip off the gown in the car as I passed the Chief Justice's house, and saw the game about to start. There was just one thing that I had forgotten.

I defy anyone - even Fred Perry himself - to reach the tramlines for Ursula Massingberd's famous overhead smash in a judge's heavy buckle shoes.

Between the two of us Lady Gawsby and I managed just three sets,   0-6, 0-6, 0-6.

CHAPTER ELEVEN

MOSHI AND THE LAW OF EVIDENCE

As I grew more accustomed to 'judicial norm' in the South Pacific British Territories, I learned to adapt English Law to outlandish conditions. Even so, it was necessary on occasions to try to draw some sort of line.

"No" I decreed, when holding court on the island of Funfati, "I'm sorry, but I cannot allow a live cobra to be exhibited in these proceedings."

The case was brought by Inspector Angus Robertson, an officer recently seconded to the South Seas from the Fifeshire Constabulary. A large man of cadaverous appearance, with an iron-grey crew cut, he had a strangely inflexible neck which always reminded me of Frankenstein's famous creation. He took out of his starched jacket pocket a black notebook from which he barked in a dour monotone the following report.

"Having myself landed in the police launch at 0600 hours on the twelfth instant, I had occasion to observe the prisoner. He was loitering at the entrance to the market-place, contrary to section 7(b) if the Vagrancy Ordinance, sub-section 1. Upon apprehending him, I saw that he had on his person a wind instrument of primitive design. Mindful of subsection 2, forbidding street music, I confiscated the aforementioned object. The prisoner insisted on putting his case in person."

I turned towards the prisoner, a scholarly looking figure with a goatee-beard, known, so I was told, as Doctor Babilu.

"The inspector did not allow time for me to explain" he protested. "I was merely getting ready for my daily work."

I adjusted my spectacles.

"What exactly is your work?" I said.

"How can I explain it to your lordship without a demonstration?"

Justice had always to be done, I reflected. I ordered Inspector Robertson to return to the defendant his musical instrument - a reed-pipe. At the same moment, Doctor Babilu slid forward a wicker basket from behind him in the dock. Raising the pipe to his mouth, he squatted down in front of the basket and blew a series of mournful notes.

Watching mesmerized, I saw the lid of the basket stir. Within seconds, the flat head of a very large snake had emerged, its forked tongue shooting out in my direction in a distinctly unfriendly fashion.

This is my partner, lordship" enthused Doctor Babilu. "She is a most fine cobra. Her name is Moshi."

It was at this point that I made my stand and ruled the reptile totally inadmissible in a British Court of Law. But the defendant proved adamant.

"This is no ordinary reptile, my lord. She is a Lambesan Cobra, specially bred by me for the destruction of cane-toads."

I felt my usual sang-froid beginning to desert me.

"Perhaps you'd better explain yourself, Doctor" I snapped.

"Certainly, my lord. My profession is that of snake charmer. Famous throughout the Southern Hemisphere."

"Indeed!"

"And now is the time of year when I make myself available to the Pacific Islanders. Otherwise their sugar-crops would be ruined by the depredations of the cane-toads."

As he spoke, I was keeping a pretty sharp eye on the heaving head with its black lidless eyes in front of me.

"Toads?!" I exclaimed. But Doctor Babilu's attention was not be distracted.

"Notice the beauty of Moshi's mottled skin, my lord" he declaimed.

A blob of perspiration fell from where my wig had slipped down to the bridge of my nose. The creature was now swaying its way uncomfortably close to the ancient deckchair from which I was presiding.

"Your lordship is in no danger" the defendant assured me with a smile. "She is knowing that I am here in control."

I indicated Doctor Babilu's pipe. "Perhaps another little tune would help" I proposed. "Music has charms and so on."

The defendant raised the pipe to his lips. At the first notes, the cobra began to sway in time. "Thus my lord, I draw her out to follow me into the cane fields or wherever she is needed. When the music stops, she returns to her basket."

The time, however, Moshi seemed reluctant to do this.

"Excuse me, lordship" said the defendant "It is Moshi's feeding time. When she has eaten, she will sleep."

"I'm afraid toad-in-the-hole is not on the court menu today" I riposted. Sometimes a joke can ease the tension in such cases.

"But Moshi can eat anything, my lord - eggs, milk, fruit, mice..."

"Mice?" I interrupted.

A sudden picture had come into my mind of their pestilential destruction of my legal tomes.

"Of course" I said "if your reptile were to perform a truly Public Service that would count in your favour."

The defendant nodded, eager to please.

"I shall need you to work with Moshi in the Court Law Library."

"But neither of us are lawyers, my lord."

One or two words of explanation were all that were needed.

Over the next couple of hours a remarkable demonstration of rodent control took place. No longer would the pages of Clarke and Lindsell on Tort, not to mention Scrutton on Charterparties, and Cheshire and Fifoot on Contract provide nourishment for the entire mouse population. Not surprisingly, by the end of the day, Moshi proved unwilling to leave.

"I shall bequeath her to your lordship" decided Doctor Babilu "in gratitude for the court's understanding."

Before leaving, the Doctor rendered Moshi's bite harmless. Harmless to humans that is. Her appetite for rodents and all other unwanted wildlife remained voracious.

As a matter of course, it was afterwards necessary for me to make up the monthly accounts. And here, admittedly, my bill to the Colonial Office met with resistance from the Audit Department at Great Smith Street, Whitehall. "Paid to Snake Charmer 500 Funfuti dollars" the item read.

"Expenditure for the private entertainment of Overseas Judges is not refundable" came the reply.

I was disappointed. After all, my own tame snake did much to improve my image with the islanders.

And even the most hardened malefactor found himself shaken from his life of crime by the flutter of Moshi's fangs and the flash of that beady black eye.

CHAPTER TWELVE

THE JUDGE'S LODGINGS

"Not J.S. again!" I sighed, when I heard from Sir Neville of my latest assignment.

Some of my encounters with this notoriously eccentric District Commissioner I have already described during my years in the South Seas. There were other bizarre incidents. How could I forget the time he landed me amongst the man-eating ray sharks of Tarawa in an effort to make the crossing before high tide, or his insistence that I perform the ritual fire walk, as his partner in full tribal dress, at the Sabusabu Banana Festival. His tall, disjointed figure with its wild thatch of white hair was a revered icon to all Micronesians. The tattered red, white and blue golfing blazer often worn with First World War army puttees made his appearance even more remarkable. But what I found particularly irritating about J.S. was his habit of making a fool of me. Not deliberately perhaps. It was just that he had a passion for converting me to whatever happened to be his current fad. On circuit to the Island of Fuam, for instance - a remote part of J.S's parish - I found the commissioner totally absorbed in his latest craze for Transcendental Meditation.

"Nothing like it my boy", he explained... He had arrived on the scene as I was trying to eat my breakfast in the Visitor's Bungalow. "A chap called Vishna is our local guru. Given me some wonderful tips."

J.S. was now sporting a dhoti borrowed from his new mentor.

"One just relaxes into the lotus position by tucking the knees firmly behind the ears." He gave an alarming demonstration. "Try it yourself."

I indicated the stack of Depositions in the Arson Trial which I had come to try.

"Must get on with these, J.S." I said.

"You'd concentrate much better if you get down to control your breathing first."

It took a lot of persuasion before J.S. agreed to leave me in peace.

Our paths crossed again at Tabuki, a former convict settlement once in French hands.

"Extraordinarily interesting, Knox Mawer. These relics of primitive gaol conditions."

I was busy taking out my robes and wig from my judicial rucksack. J.S. however was preoccupied with his own bag of tricks.

"Just try on these pinion-irons, old boy" he said. "Give you an idea what convicts had to put up with in those days."

Before I could stop him, J.S. had snapped onto me a pair of ankle-cuffs. A Guard of Honour of the Tabuki Constabulary was drawn up outside the thatched courthouse, waiting for me to inspect them.

"I seem to have mislaid the key, old chap" murmured J.S. He began to rummage through a rusty pile of prison chains. "You just carry on though - until I find the damn thing."

Carry on! Did he think I could inspect his bloody parade in a series of hops, like some sort of legal kangaroo?! It was lucky that my extreme shortage of muscle in the calves allowed me to wriggle free. Without J.S's assistance.

All in all I found myself wondering if the man was altogether sane. Certainly the authorities made sure he was stationed in the most out of the way territories. This meant that I was able to go for long periods without meeting him.

In fact I had more or less succeeded in putting J.S. out of my mind. This made Sir Neville's unexpected directive all the more of a shock.

In vain, I pleaded a sudden attack of dysentery - "requiring a bit of hospital treatment, sir."

My Chief Justice remained unmoved:"District Commissioner J.S. Pennington has specifically requested your urgent services, Knox Mawer, on the island of Waini Bokasi. And that's that."

As I was soon to learn, the crisis this time concerned what are known as the Judges Lodgings. In the home country, a visiting Assize Judge is accommodated with all due comfort at public expense in a suitably staffed country mansion. Not so in far flung Polynesia.

J.S. greeted my judicial launch at the Waini Bokasi Wharf with a flourish of his ancient panama.

"You may find the Judges Lodgings here a bit odder than usual."

"How exactly do you mean?"

"Happens to be a Tree House."

"A Tree House?!"

"Provided the Hurricane Season doesn't break, I think you'll be perfectly comfortable" he went on.

"I can't possibly..."

"Nonsense. It's a great honour. Surely you remember that our own revered monarch occupied a famous Tree House in Kenya, just before she became Queen.."

For a moment, I was reassured, until J.S. continued "As you would expect in the South Seas, these structures are more primitive."

Surrounded by enthusiastic locals in leafy skirts and garlands, we were now making our way through the mangrove swamp at the edge of the beach. J.S. pointed ahead to the shape of a vast gloomy tree on the edge of the village.

"It's in there, originally constructed for the High Priest of the tribe. He was the guardian of the sacred bats who inhabit the tree, you understand."

"Bats!" I exclaimed..

"Flying foxes is the name of that particular species. Quite large as a matter of fact. Rare of course. Your predecessor particularly enjoyed their company. But there again, Rob Garfield was something of an amateur zoologist,"

"Well I'm not" I said, defiantly.

"That can't be helped. You'll soon get used to them. And remember it's your duty to respect the bats because they are believed to embody the spirits of departed elders."

"Are they indeed?" I said.

By now, we were standing at the base of a large banyan tree. Peering up the branches, I could see an elaborate platform affair, thatched and screened with coconut matting.

"How do I get up there?"

J.S. pointed to a ladder made of plaited sinnet. "Leave your briefcase and goloshes with me and grab hold of Lord Kitchener's hand when you get near the top."

"Who?"

"Lord Kitchener. Adopted name of my senior domestic. Fine athlete. Won the marathon at the South Pacific Games. He's on loan to you, awaiting your arrival. Your batman so to speak."

The ascent proved fairly straight forward, except that mildew had so rotted my court striped trousers that the seat developed an embarrassing split when put under strain. With Lord Kitchener's assistance, however, I managed to scramble through the foliage as J.S. boomed up another direction.

"Whatever you do, don't disturb Vandalu."

"Vandalu?"

"He's the monarch of the bat world. Sleeps just above your head."

I can't say that I welcomed the company of this umbrella-shaped creature barely a foot away. Even so, I did my best to make myself at home, despite the comings and goings of Vandalu's retinue throughout the night. Lord Kitchener had produced a hammock and mosquito net and I'd managed to discover a useful nook for my sponge bag and dressing gown.

I read myself to sleep by the light of a hurricane lamp with Volume Three of the Memoirs of Sir Arthur Gordon, Governor of Fiji in the eighteen-seventies. In an address to the Polynesian Society, Sir Arthur had pointed out that a chief would never bivouac at ground level.

"The position of the head" Sir Arthur had declared "is of enormous significance in Oceanic Society. One of higher rank must never allow the head of a lesser personage to be raised above his own."   He certainly would have approved of me, perched some thirty feet above the village rooftops, I thought to myself, as I eventually closed my eyes.

J.S. was still on the same subject when I tottered down the next morning.

"So do try to straighten up, old chap. That stoop of yours has got considerably worse since I last saw you. And bear in mind that like Lord Kitchener there's hardly an islander under six foot."

"I'll do my best" I said.

"Anyway" he continued "I've arranged for four of the tallest warriors to carry you overhead to the Court House. So that should solve the problem to a certain extent."

My litter was made out of pandanus leaves and resembled a gigantic pram.

"It's a wonder you haven't supplied me with a dummy and rattle" I quipped feebly, as they bore me aloft.

"Now you come to mention it" said J.S. "you are missing something..."

Before taking his place at the front of the procession, he signalled to the leader. The next minute I was handed a fly whisk and a drinking-coconut.

"All part of the service" J.S. declared.

With a drummer beating on a wooden drum behind us, our little cortege arrived at the Meeting Hall, where I was to hold sessions. There was a slight problem when it came to transferring me from the "pram" onto the Bench. But, with the skills of the natural rugby players, my bearers slipped me deftly over the heads of the onlookers. The bamboo Seat of Justice itself, sited under the palm roof, was suitably elevated.

"I've stacked your set of Halsbury's Laws of England under the legs" said J.S. "Just to give it that extra bit of height."

"How on earth am I going to manage if I wish to refer to one of the volumes upon a point of law?" I asked.

J.S. guffawed. "For a case involving two missing crabpots!" he scorned.

In point of fact, J.S. was far too dismissive of my Cause List. There was a difficult summons involving a prisoner released from the island jail. He had caused criminal damage by endeavouring to break back in again. He claimed that he had been invited by the jailer, his cousin, to a Prison Jambouree and that the damage was purely accidental.

"Right-ho there, old boy" interrupted J.S. I was recording the jailer's evidence in my usual careful way. "I'm off into the Bush. See you in a couple of days."

It was highly irresponsible of J.S. not to warn me of a delicate predicament which lay ahead. I was pronouncing judgement in a case at the end of the Assize Sitting. Between Waini Bokasi and the neighbouring island of Kavalu was a tiny strip of sand, where turtles were easily taken by fishermen. After studying the relevant maps, I ruled that the people of the neighbouring island were entitled to the turtle haul and *not* the Waini Bokasan islanders. No sooner had I announced my decision, than I was surrounded by rioting Waini Bokasan islanders. This was not the time for standing on any kind of ceremony. I was only too happy to be hustled back to the Judge's Lodging, where Lord Kitchener managed to get me up the rope ladder at speed.

THE SIEGE OF THE TREEHOUSE became a part of the Waini Bokasi legend, although it lasted no longer than a day.

"What would you have done if you hadn't our unique Judge's Lodgings to retreat to?!" chaffed Pennington, upon his return from safari.

It was with some relief however when J.S. saw me safely off in the Judicial Launch. As we made our way down the beach, a number of my overnight companions followed us, flapping and squeaking at my shoulder.

"They seem to have become quite attached to you" said J.S.

"The things we do for Queen and Country" I groaned, as I lunged across into the boat. "The Colonial Authorities are never going to believe it."

J.S. gave me an affectionate poke with his huge gnarled walking stick.

"Never mind" he called over the waves. "Just tell them you were batting for England!"

CHAPTER THIRTEEN

THE GHOST OF BOW STREET

Cricketing metaphors had a tiresome way of dogging my career.

"So now you're stumped!" observed Austin Bolsover Q.C. on my return to the U.K. a few months later.

We had once been fellow pupils at the Inns of Court. Hearing that I was home for a spot of leave he had invited me to lunch in the Inner Temple.

"Stumped for a job I mean" he went on, seeing my blank expression.

"Well it's not that bad" I said. "Although since the South Sea Islanders have become self-governing all that's on offer for me is a short-term contract."

Austin helped himself to another enormous glass of port.

"Happens that I'm on the Judicial Appointments Committee here in London" he said.

He made his way through a wedge of stilton after opening another button of his Saville Row waistcoat.

"It's just possible there might be an opening for you laddie as a Metropolitan Stipendiary Magistrate".

I knew of course that the London Beaks, as the Metropolitan Magistrates were called, numbered about fifty salaried lawyers whose job was to cope with inner-city crime at street level.

"But would I be in the running?"

"Well after 15 years of jungle-judging, laddie, you should have earned yourself a good mark or two. And there's sometimes room on the Metropolitan Bench for an oddball."

Bolsover was on his feet before I could say anything.

"Got to dash. Conference with the Attorney General."

I never did find out what Austin Bolsover did on my behalf. Certainly his Whitehall cronies were nothing if not cautious.

"Try him out in the provinces first," they decided.

I was sent to deputise for the Merseyside Stipendiary Magistrate during the winter of powercuts.

FROM BALI-HI TO BIRKENHEAD read a short paragraph in the Liverpool Daily Post .

FORMER SOUTH SEA STIPENDIARY SHIVERS IN THE SNOW.

The appalling contrast in temperature had obliged me to sit on the Bench in a heavy overcoat, muffler and gloves.

"Court to break for five minutes" I announced. It was ice-cold in the Retiring Room. I was trying to get the circulation into my feet by stamping up and down when the telephone rang.

"Bolsover here" boomed his voice in my ear "Good news old sport. They've approved your London Appointment."

"Great."

"They need to have your present postal address. Based somewhere in North Wales aren't you? Nobody seems too sure of the exact address."

"Yes. Three miles out of Llangollen as a matter of fact. My cottage is called Fron Fawr, Eglwyseg."

"Spell that out again, for God's sake."

"Well just put ' Worlds End' " I said, "that's the name of the particular Llangollen district where I'm to be found."

"Very appropriate," chortled Bolsover before ringing off.

Two weeks later a red sealed envelope was left for me by the postman on the usual empty milk churn at the end of Fron Fawr Lane.

"Please report to the Chief Metropolitan Stipendiary Magistrate, Sir Robert Mildmay at Bow Street Court forthwith" it read.

My first day in the stately Victorian building opposite Covent Garden was spent on the top floor in what was known as The

New Beak's Court. I was entrusted only with minor pavement offences and infringement of the traffic regulations. At the close of the afternoon session my departure via the back stairs was interrupted by the Chief Magistrate's usher. He explained that Sir Robert wished to see me,

"Anything wrong , sir?" I enquired, peering anxiously around the imposing door of the Chief Magistrate's Chambers.

"Not that I am aware of" came the guarded reply.

He motioned for me to take a seat.

"It's just that I want you to be on hand this evening, to meet up with Wally, our handyman" he said.

From the mantelpiece behind his desk Sir Robert took down a sketch.

"I'm going to have a temporary seating extension for the dock knocked up in Court Number One. There's several hundred demonstrators due to appear before me after trouble in Trafalgar Square."

The usher tiptoed in carrying a silver tray with coffee.

"Help yourself" said Sir Robert as the usher pushed firmly in my direction the cup without a judicial crest.

Sir Robert turned his attention to some urgent papers and I sneaked a glance around. In a central position on the wall was a gold-lettered board, listing the names of the Chief Magistrate's predecessors, with Henry Fielding, the author of Tom Jones, at the top. Alongside was a striking portrait of a burly figure in eighteenth century coat, breeches and tricorn hat, carrying a staff. MR. TOWNSEND THE FIRST BOW STREET RUNNER read the caption. I felt like doing a runner myself.

"Now this is what I have in mind" said Sir Robert, tapping the plan with the side of his gold-rimmed spectacles. "Wally's coming in at seven. So familiarise yourself with what's needed and make sure you're on hand at that time."

With a brisk glance at his pocket watch, Sir Robert moved off to take the Daily Cause List. Dusk had fallen, and the chief had long since left the building when I made my way into his court. It was a large cavernous arena with lamps which were none too bright. A wind was blowing the rain against the glass 1882 cupola, high above my head.

As I waited, I was joined by Mr. Albert Crouch, the Collector of Fines.

"Been here since 1929 man and boy," explained Mr. Crouch. Despite his venerable age, he was quick and spry.

"Care for a little conducted tour, sir?" he said, "seeing that you're half an hour early."

"Thank you Mr. Crouch," I agreed, hurrying to catch up with him as he moved across from the witness box and the various enclosures for counsel, for solicitors, for the press, and for the probation officers. He walked with a jaunty hop like a sparrow.

"Not that I've ever seen anything myself," he confided, as we stood under the EXIT sign," but this is the Court room that's supposed to be haunted.

"Who by?"

"That's just the point sir. Nobody seems to know."

I followed Mr. Crouch down to the cells.

"There's been some rum characters through these lock-ups," he said. Each cell contained a hard wooden seat and a tiny opening for air.

"Oakley the poisoner I remember in my early days. Pasty faced chap with one eye."

"I suppose the spook could be a woman," I suggested.

"Maybe sir. There was Maudie Price, the fraudulent medium. Looked just like a witch I've heard. Arrested under the old law against the casting of evil spells."

Together we returned to Mr. Crouch's office where he offered me a glass of sherry.

"My money would be on Lurkan, the Clerkenwell Strangler. Horrible monster. Some reckoned he was Jack the Ripper."

When I made my way back to the dock of Court Number One there was still no sign of Wally. I glanced at the ornate clock above the mahogany notice-board. He was already ten minutes late. Examining the dock from the inside was an eerie experience. Several of the spectral candidates discussed with Albert Crouch flashed through my mind. Perched against the iron grill with my head in my hands, I was roused by a sudden clatter. Someone had dropped a bucket high up in the gallery behind me. It was followed by a loud female shriek.

"Inspector Brown! Inspector Brown!" The piercing voice floated down to me. "I just see'd 'im! That bleedin' ghost they keeps talking about!"

I caught a glimpse of a small stout figure scuttling out of the gallery, in search of the Court Inspector. In the shadowy gloom, it was difficult to see clearly, but the lady in distress was evidently the cleaner.

"Calm yourself Mrs Floyd" someone called through the grill of the Fines Collection Office, just behind.

"Calm myself Inspector?!   After seeing that 'orrible maniac with me own eyes!"

The voices died away. The door was slammed behind them and I heard no more until, five minutes later, Inspector Brown himself came down into the court.

"Our cleaning lady Mrs Floyd is in a bit of a state of shock, sir."

"What seems to be the trouble, officer?"

"Says she's seen a ghost in the dock. Perhaps you'd be kind enough to explain the mistake to her. She's having a mug of tea in the office at the moment."

"I'm afraid I don't follow you."

The Inspector paused.

"Well - er - you, in your black jacket, and it being a bit on the shady side in here."

He coughed politely.

"And if you don't mind my saying so, you are looking rather under the weather. With that gastric 'flu bug you were telling me about earlier."

He was looking at me most considerately.

"Not that I would say there was any resemblance though."

"Resemblance, officer?"

I was even more confused.

"To Doctor Crippen, the famous wife-murderer, sir. That's who Mrs Floyd reckons she's seen, believe it or not."   Crippen was not one of the candidate ghosts mentioned by Mr. Crouch.

I sighed. "As a matter of fact, Inspector, I do feel a bit groggy" I said "where's the nearest W.C.?"

"Sir Robert's private convenience is just down the corridor, sir."

The Chief Magistrate's cloakroom was not exactly a welcoming place, with its dark mahogany fittings and enormously high and intimidating Gothic ceiling. The lamp in the gas-mantle shed a meagre light on the ancient marble wash bowl. Surveying myself in the mottled looking-glass above, I was rather taken aback by the deathly pallor of my features. Nor did the design of the lavatory itself offer comfort. The giant polished seat was even icier than it looked. And from the rusted iron canopy overhead there hung a pull-chain the length of a hangman's noose. I was anxious to leave as quickly as I could.

"I tried to tell her that it was you, the new stipendiary magistrate, she'd seen" the Inspector went on, as I rejoined him on the stairs "but she won't have it. Bit of a theatrical disposition has Mrs Floyd. Perhaps it comes from that other cleaning job of hers. at the Opera House, over the way. Sort of mixing you up with the Phantom of the Opera."

By the time Wally arrived, Mrs Floyd had fled. She left behind her mop and bucket, and a half-smoked cigarette, stained with magenta lipstick. I rapidly dealt with Wally and the plan for additional seating in the dock, before making my departure.

 I must have been in a state of confusion because I caught the wrong bus home, and ended up at the Golders Green Crematorium, not a place I would choose for my evening destination.

Subsequently I made a point of leaving the premises promptly after work - good cleaners being hard to find. But one day, I had to collect some documents from the Chief's court-room. It was after sunset and I thought I saw something like a shadow, moving in the dock. It looked like a small man in glasses. Probably just a trick of the light, I told myself. There was a funny smell, however, which was not very pleasant. That must surely have been the rotten wood, uncovered in the course of other alterations. It also seemed very cold in there. I made a note to get Wally back. Just to check up on the heating that is.

CHAPTER FOURTEEN

AN INTERRUPTION FROM THE PAST

I recognised the writing immediately. J.S. Pennington's spidery crawl was unmistakable. His missive was addressed and delivered to me - c/o Bow Street Court W.C.1. on August 3rd.

"Fancy the old boy remembering my birthday after all these years" was my first thought. What I'd forgotten was J.S.'s notorious addiction to schoolboy pranks, something he shared with Father's adversary Hurford Jenkins. I should have guessed that the envelope might conceal something unexpected. There was a sudden pop as the tiny BILLY BUNTER STINK BOMB exploded onto my blotter releasing a particularly embarrassing smell into the stately corridors of justice. This was a sulphurous compound associated with the passing of wind that had always been a source of merriment to the spotty adolescents illustrated on the pages of the pre-war Boys Magazine The Magnet,

"Usher!"   The voice of my Head barked out from the adjoining chambers "what on earth is that disgusting odour?!"

"Could be the drains again, Sir Robert," I heard the faint voice of the Usher reply.

"Something a damn sight worse this time. Send for the plumber at once!"

There was no alternative but for me to hurry in to the learned Chief Magistrate and try to explain the situation.

"It's just something absurd sent to me by an ex-colleague of mine in the Colonial Service sir. Rather an eccentric I'm afraid. He thinks this sort of thing is funny sir."

"He's a bloody lunatic if you ask me."

I could not help agreeing with Sir Robert as I returned to my own desk while the usher disposed of the debris and opened the window to let in some fresh air.

"Many Happy Returns" J.S. had written upon the accompanying note. "Here's hoping that your new position doesn't mean that you've lost your sense of humour!"

J.S. was now himself retired back in the U.K. Under his signature he had given a telephone number which I crossly dialled, there and then, to give him a piece of my mind.

'He's got to realise that we're no longer in the South Seas,' I told myself. Upon no account was I prepared to tolerate J.S.'s brand of infantile tomfoolery. Not in the Home Country.

"Miss Gertrude Pennington speaking," answered a haughty voice at the end of the line.

I tried to explain the reason for my call but was sharply interrupted.

"The number you have dialled is Starkboulder Hall, the Pennington home in North Yorkshire. It must be my brother you want to speak to."

"How are the Bow Street Runners, old boy?" came J.S.'s cheery boom as he took up the receiver.

"I'm not in the mood for chit-chat, J.S.", I told him, putting him quickly in the picture.

"So sorry I've caused you embarrassment my lad," he laughed in that maddening way of his.

There was a pause and I heard him strike a match and light up.

"The pipe of peace? Alright?"

I remained silent.

"Where are you staying by the way," he enquired.

"No base so far," I answered testily.

"Well I can do you a good turn on that score," he said. "Happens that I own a little pad near Trafalgar Square. How would it suit you for a while. Give you a chance to look around."

"Well it would be nice to be near the court while I see a couple of Estate Agents" I told J.S. "What about you though?"

"I certainly won't be going down for a couple of months," he said "the grouse season and all that. You can pick up the keys at the Royal Empire Society, Northumberland Avenue."

I took J.S. at his word and called there immediately after work.

"Somebody's already taken Mr. Pennington's keys, sir" I was told at the R.E.S. Puzzled, I decided upon a spot of reconnaissance. What kind of flat exactly was it? I wondered. And who'd got the key?

Following my A-Z, I made my way through the dusty side-streets at the back of theatre land until I found number 86 Soho Square. The front door seemed to have had the paint kicked away at the bottom. Under Bell Push 5 was the name Pennington. I tried one or two of the others and eventually somebody buzzed the entry phone to let me in. Pennington's door at the top of the last flight of rickety stairs was open. Strange I thought.

Once inside, the scene that confronted me defied description. It was as though a Tropical Hurricane had swept through. The carpet was badly churned up, with torn cushions heaped in piles around. There were empty whisky bottles everywhere and dozens of squashed lager cans. I picked my way through a minefield of cardboard containers holding the remnants of takeaway Chinese and Indian food, before tripping over a guitar with broken strings. The waste disposal unit in the kitchen was jammed with an enormous studded boot.

I had seen enough.

"I'm ringing on the telephone in your flat, J.S." I snapped "heaven knows what the devil's been going on here."

I gave J.S. a brief run-down of the scene.

"Oh yes laddie" he chuckled "I quite forgot. I told my friends in the Polynesian rugby team that they could make use of the place if they were stuck over accommodation. They've obviously been celebrating that splendid victory at Twickenham.. Given a bit more time, their captain Jo Pacifica would have left the place spotless. You can always rely on old Jo."

"Not this time" I said "there's no sign of him."

"Are you sure? There must be a message. Have another look round."

This time I looked into the bathroom.

"If you mean that great hulking fellow in the bath with a paper hat on his head, yes, the great man is here in person but not exactly compos mentis. Obviously the rest of the team have made off."

I removed a large piece of curried chipatti from my heel.

"Really J.S., this situation is the last straw!"

"I do think you're making an awful lot of fuss about nothing, Knox-Mawer," he replied. "You've helped me over a bit of a hangover many a time. Get cracking my boy, and do the same thing for Jo."

I sighed.

Better try to get Jo on his way I decided. I picked up the telephone again. "So long as you don't expect me to tackle this shambles on my own afterwards," I stipulated.

"For goodness sake, K.M., you're getting free accommodation! Surely that's the least you can do in return."

He rang off, leaving me to cope.

After filling Captain Pacifica with black coffee I somehow managed to get him safely into a taxi. I then returned to J.S's living room and set about collecting the junk into rubbish bags. It was hard going. I knew more than most about the exhuberance of these delightful South Pacific Islanders. In other circumstances I would have been only too happy to join in their celebrations. But this was altogether different.

And then again, quite apart from the Rugby Team's left-overs, the flat itself was hardly a normal habitation. There were distinct echoes of J.S's run-down Commissioner's Bungalow on the beach at Sabu sabu. Amongst J.S's makeshift bark cloth curtains and the tribal carvings that propped up his bookshelf, the Polynesians had naturally felt at home. There was even an oil lamp hanging from the ceiling. Presumably for J.S's use when the electricity bills had not been paid. I removed a grass skirt from what looked like a bird-cage in the corner of the dining room.

"Gar-out! Gar-out! Gar-out!" squawked a large green Noumean parrot. I might have guessed that J.S's long-time travelling companion would be in residence. Henry seemed to have plenty of food and water but was obviously irritated at being disturbed from his sleep.

Replacing the skirt, I resumed my efforts. As I trundled back and to with brush and pan, it began to strike me as a hopeless task. What a fool I'd been to imagine that anything connected with J.S. would not end up in disaster.

Just then the telephone rang again.

"It's the Westminster Health Inspector here" said a voice "a serious complaint has been received from neighbours in the flats adjoining yours. Concerning noise and other environmental problems. I'm coming there to see for myself."

The phone went down.

Obviously there was no time for a getaway. I reached out for the nearest bottle with anything left in it, - vodka as it turned out. I took a few large swigs, greatly restoring my morale by the time the front door buzzer went. When I opened up to the Health Inspector he reeled back at the sight of the chaos behind me.

"I can explain everything, Inspector," I began.

A short spectacled man, in an official uniform, he immediately brought out his notebook.

"There can't be any explanation for this sort of thing, can there sir?" he said. "So if you'll just let me step inside I can get on with my report."

It was difficult to clarify the situation in a few gabbled words.

"I should put that bottle down if I were you sir," he said. The Inspector's mood was becoming brusque.

"Name and occupation first if you please."

I hesitated. Then drew myself up.

"Former Chief Justice of Tavioni and Futilevu," I said more distinctly "now occupying the Metropolitan Bench at Bow Street. Name is Knox Mawer R."

The Inspector gave a violent start, the kind one sees in a B. movie.

"Sorry sir" he gasped. "But I thought I'd seen you before. It was you that signed the Entry Warrant for me to go into a condemned property in Temple Bar. Are you here on an official visit, your worship?"

"Hardly" I said. "But come to think of it there's no reason why I shouldn't be."

On the instant I made a decision. It was high-time that the particular owner of these unhygienic premises was made to take his responsibility as a London Resident seriously.

"Sorry? How exactly do you mean sir?"

"Well the owner is somebody I know all too well. Indeed he went so far as to suggest that I might wish to come into occupation. In point of fact I have only been here ten minutes."

In response to my invitation to continue his exploration of the flat the inspector tried to open the bedroom door. Only to be drowned in an avalanche of old copies of the Fiji Times.

"A bit of a drop-out is he sir, this acquaintance of yours?"

"You could say that."

"If you give me the necessary details as to who and where he's to be found sir, I'll set the necessary procedures in motion."

My hesitation was only momentary. "The name and address, Inspector, is care of J.S. Pennington, Starkboulder Hall, North Yorkshire."

After all, I told myself, J.S. always reckoned to enjoy a surprise. "At any time of the night or day, old boy."

This should be one he would remember.

CHAPTER FIFTEEN

MARYLEBONE

"Could I have a word with you, Knox Mawer?"

I jumped. It was the voice of the Chief Magistrate, Sir Robert Mildmay, arriving unexpectedly early in his Chambers. Was he about to interrogate me about the reprehensible conduct of my one-time colleague J.S. Pennington?! I hurried out of the Library to obey the summons.

Inside his room, Sir Robert was already hunched over his desk, his bald head glinting in the morning sun.

"I want you to do a bit of floating" he observed, without looking up.

"Sorry sir?"

"Do you know your way about Central London yet?"

"I'm doing my best."

"Well take the tube to Baker Street, turn left until you come to a building bearing the plaque" - his voice rose to a boom as if I was somehow deaf.

"MARYLEBONE PUBLIC SWIMMING BATHS."

"Did you say Public Baths sir?" I ventured.

"That's right. Can't miss 'em. Most impressive bit of architecture in Marylebone Road."

Sir Robert adjusted his pince-nez.

"I've decided the best way is to throw you in at the deep end. Sink or swim, you might say."

I gaped. Was the whole thing some public school ritual of initiation for new recruits in the Metropolitan system?

Sir Robert's features remained impassive. Then with a glimmer of a smile, he relented.

"Perhaps I should explain that the building was converted into a police court during the war. Just my little joke, you know."

That was a relief anyway. Even so, what exactly was all this about 'floating'?

"You'll be acting as leave-relief for your colleagues" he explained. "In departmental terms you'll be what we call a floater. So you'll be spending a fortnight at one court, where the incumbent is on holiday and then you'll move on to the next one, as the holiday rota dictates." He chuckled. "We appreciate that working on the Inner London Bench is very different from your Jungle Judging. But we're hoping you'll adjust to it."

Still somewhat confused, I set off as instructed. I must have emerged from the Tube at the wrong end, because I suddenly found myself outside Madame Tussauds in the queue for the Chamber of Horrors. A traffic warden came to my rescue.

"That's the Marylebone Court" she said, pointing to the corner of Seymour Place. "It's the backdoor for Parking Fines."

I tried a bell marked CHIEF CLERK without success, then managed to gain admittance through the public entrance. Inside, an ancient notice board marked Bastardy Applications greeted me.

"Marylebone moves with the times" I quipped to the uniformed janitor behind the hatch. He remained unmoved.

My chambers turned out to be large and dusty, with a huge desk in the centre and a shelf of out-of-date Stones Justices Manuals by the window behind. The in-tray contained a vast pile of committal warrants, with nothing in the out-tray apart from a stained coffee cup with a broken handle. In the far corner was a wardrobe, empty save for an enormous pair of galoshes.

"Property of Colonel Batt."

A ramrod figure in a black jacket and pinstripe trousers had stepped in behind me, giving me a start.

"Hector McVie, Principal Chief Clerk" he barked by way of introduction "generally known in the Service as Principal McVie." Briskly he closed the wardrobe door on the galoshes. "The Colonel left them behind when he retired as Resident Stipendiary. Been there ever since. They'll not be collected now."

"You never know" I said. "He may surprise us one day."

"Some surprise alright" said   Principal McVie grimly. "Colonel Batt died five years ago."

Upon the opposite wall to the window was a large signed photograph of Kind Edward V11th.

"It was presented by His Majesty when he officially opened the Baths. Miss Knowles was very proud of it" explained the Principal..

"Miss Knowles?"

"Yes. This was her room. She was a famous personage here. Matron Superintendent of Ablutions for the Unwashed Poor."

"Dear me" I said. "Thank goodness those days have gone."

Again Mr. McVie gave the same sinister smile. "You'll still find plenty of unwashed customers awaiting your attention."

He consulted a gold pocket watch.

"Time to make a start" he announced. "Essential to get at them right on the dot."

He led the way along a narrow corridor. He had a severely cropped neck, which seemed to pulsate with a manic energy of its own. Not for nothing I discovered, was he known as the Genghis Khan of the Inner London Courts Service.

After ascending several wooden steps, we entered the court-room from behind the Bench. The conversion of what had been a High Diving Pool had apparently been done in a hurry during the wartime emergency. Consequently, despite the usual judicial fittings, the arena still had the dank echoing atmosphere of a Municipal Bath. There was also a strange hissing sound that seemed to come from the heating system. This was interrupted at intervals by various flushings and gurglings coming from somewhere underground. As a result, the acoustics were appalling. Colonel Batt had tried to overcome this difficulty by having a microphone system installed. However, when Mr. McVie switched on this apparatus, I was deafened by a loud whistling, like a badly tuned wireless set.

"Best to do without it, Mr. McVie" I suggested.

Apart from the difficulty of hearing what was going on in the case before me, I was having an embarrassing time with the seating arrangements. The Magistrate's Chair was an elaborate structure of wrought iron. Unfortunately the leather seat was unevenly worn so that the supporting springs were at different levels. As a result I found myself thrown off balance from time to time.

I was trying to cope with this problem when a Railway Official, carrying his gold-braided cap, stepped into the witness box.

"Marylebone Ticket Inspector" called out the Principal. "He is applying for 343 summonses for evasion of fares, sir."

"Could I have your name please?" I enquired.

Leaning forward, I heard a spring give way. At the same moment, my left knee somehow became trapped between the drawers under the Bench. Inadvertently, I let out a faint shriek.

"Anything wrong?" called up Mr. McVie, in an irritated voice.

"Nothing much. Though I would suggest a replacement of the magistrate's seating arrangements as soon as is possible."

"The colonel never complained" observed Mr. McVie.

I repositioned myself as well as I could for the next case, having dealt against the odds with the Ticket Inspector's application. After a quick search through the cupboards an ancient air cushion was found. Thus equipped I readied myself for the next application.

"Mr. Solomon Abrahams, of the Marlborough Arms, wishes to transfer his licence to Vijay Patel" said Principal McVie.

Once on the witness stand, Mr. A. correctly placed upon his head the trilby kept for the taking of the oath by those of the Jewish persuasion. Next into the box was Mr. Patel himself. Before we could stop him, he also clamped the hat on his head. Obviously he imagined it to be part of the judicial ritual.

"I am Hindu" he announced.

"In that case, Mr. Patel" I explained "You'll not be needing the hat. Just your own holy book for the oath, if you please."

This was duly supplied, and all went well,.

For the next two hours, Mr. McVie took me through the Morning Schedule at a ruthless pace. There was a large number of remands - robberies and muggings, where the defendants had to be committed for trial at the Old Bailey, or returned to Brixton until the police inquiries were finally completed.

"Alfred Hitchens, arrested for non-payment of fines, totalling three hundred and seventy pounds, for joyriding offences" announced the Principal.

A peaky youth in a torn T-shirt surfaced in the dock.

"Nothing whatsoever paid" said Mr. McVie "the alternative is six weeks imprisonment."

"Giv' us a chance, Gov" said Hitchens.

"He's already been given several chances to pay" said Mr. McVie "all to no effect whatsoever. And he's arrived here in a brand new motor car if you like!"

"The Motor Car" I mused. "That fetish of Western Culture! Rather similar to the Boar's Tusk universally prized in Eastern Micronesia."

The young man nodded dumbly. Mr. McVie gave the file an exasperated rattle.

"The car outside is me muvver's sir" continued Hitchens, sensing sympathy on my part. "She borrowed it, see, so as I could get 'er mixture from the chemist. She's got terrible rheumatics, sir. That's where me dole money'd gone, paying for 'er mixture."

"There might be something in this, Mr. McVie" I said.

"A pack of lies, in my view" said the learned Principal.

"Me uncle wot lent the motor's got a shop in Edgware Road. Just round the corner, Gov" interjected Hitchens "promised to lend me the cash 'e has."

"Another tall one, no doubt" rasped Mr. McVie.

"Just let me free to nip round there, Gov. Promise I'll be back in five minutes with the money."

"Most unwise" advised Mr. McVie "a youth with a bad criminal record."

"Well I think the lad should be given a final opportunity to pay up" I said, allowing Hitchens to be released. An hour passed. There was no sign of Hitchens.

"The Warrant Officer reports that, exactly as I predicted, the prisoner has scarpered" said Mr. McVie. "The car he arrived in proves to be a stolen vehicle. Worse still, he's parked it behind my own vehicle, taking with him the ignition keys!"

I issued a warrant for Kitchens' arrest and adjourned for lunch. The situation was particularly galling for Mr. McVie.

"No replacement ignition key can be obtained in under two hours" he complained.

This meant that due to my misguided act of trust he had to forego his usual lunch, - vegetarian I gathered, and slavishly prepared each day by Mrs McVie in their St. John's Wood flat.

Nor did I endear myself to Principal McVie at the end of the afternoon session.

"Just two matters have come in for disposal" he explained.

In the first, the defendant pleaded guilty to interrupting a cricket match at Lords, by running naked onto the pitch. In the second, a doleful individual in an old raincoat admitted that he had exposed his person in Regent's Park, to an unappreciative group of Japanese lady tourists.

"Colonel Batt never wasted words on these types" advised Mr. McVie. "Quick sharp spells of custody are the only answer."

"One needs a degree of reflection here" I observed. "After all, over boastful demonstrations of masculinity prevail worldwide. In Northern Borneo, for instance, I myself discovered this. No doubt, Dr. Sigmund Freud would say ..." I went on, only to be cut short as Mr. McVie slammed down the Register. The combination of a streaker a flasher and a floater was all to much for him.

Summing up, I adjourned both these cases for psychiatric reports.

"Best to try to look into the medical background and attendant circumstances" I decided.

Back in chambers, with the day's work over, I invited Mr. McVie to join me for coffee.

He was clearly impatient to go. He directed a meaningful glance at the clock, which showed half-past seven.

"We've always finished the work here at five, at the very latest" he pointed out. With military precision he adjusted his grey tartan scarf. "As a matter of fact I was planning a few days off. Next month" he said.

He picked up his bowler and flicked off a speck of dust. "However I've changed my plan." He strode briskly towards the door. "I shall be starting my leave tomorrow. A fishing lodge in the Outer Hebrides."

The door closed behind his final piece of information.

"No telephone of course."

CHAPTER SIXTEEN

LAMBETH

Just when I had become adjusted to the vagaries of Marylebone, word came that I was to be floated on to Lambeth. The only information given was that the Police Court there was just a short walk from the Elephant and Castle Underground Station.

"Thought they'd closed the place down" said the ticket collector pointing me in the right direction. It certainly looked that way. The iron railings around the small brick and stone court building were choked with nettles. Nobody answered the bell at the side door marked MAGISTRATE. As I reached the front steps, a bent figure in a tattered black gown appeared at the top.

"Would you be Mr. Knox-Mawer, sir?"

"Not if I could help it" I felt like replying.

"Perkins is the name, sir. Court Keeper."

He conducted me into a musty back room and switched on the light. A mug and plate on the table indicated that he had just finished his breakfast.

"Would you please let the staff know that I'm here" I said.

"I am the staff, sir" he replied.

I blinked.

"Arthur Baxter, the young deputy clerk, has rung in to say that he's broken down outside New Cross. Says we can carry on until he gets the car mended."

"Not too happy about that" I said.

"There's only odds and sods on your list, sir" was the Keeper's reply.

"I don't follow you" I said coldly.

"Well it's only when a Stipendiary's got nothing better to do, sir, that he's sent to Lambeth."

"Is that so!"

"Not a regular court any longer sir" explained Mr. Perkins. "Only takes the left-overs. Nothing that's urgent if you understand me sir."

"Every case is urgent to those involved in it, Mr. Perkins" I snapped.

"I'm sure you're right, sir" he said dolefully. "But that's how it's regarded."

Now I came to think about it I remembered a strange remark made by Principal Hector McVie about Lambeth being "our judicial lumber room." I was beginning to see what he meant, although if struck me as a pretty poor use of my experience on the Overseas Bench, whichever way one looked at it.

Meanwhile the Keeper seemed ready to start the day's proceedings.

"If you'll bear with me a minute, sir I'll see if anybody's turned up".

With a tortoise-like movement he pushed his head through a door on the opposite side of the room, marked COURT.

"Yes sir, it's the Daley and Brewster case." He brushed away a stray crumb from the front of his gown. "Been adjourned on and off for years."

I straightened my tie and gave Perkins a quick nod.

"Watch that hole in the carpet sir" he warned as he proceeded ahead of me.

"All silent" he called our - a totally unnecessary command as the courtroom was deserted.

"The parties are outside in the passageway, your worship" explained the Keeper.

I stumbled over an unforseen extra step.

"Am I expected to work in the dark, Mr. Perkins?" I complained. The feeble ray of light from the latticed window set high above the Bench was of little help.

"I was just looking in to the fuse box" said Mr. Perkins. "The bulb over your desk has blown but I've got a three amp replacement that should do for now. I'm afraid the London Electricity Board has warned us of repairs, so power is low."

The whole arrangement struck me as exceedingly primitive especially as Mr. Perkins was hopelessly short of spares. But there was no point in getting hot under the collar. Worse was to come, however. When Perkins had succeeded in putting on the main switches, I experienced a moment of eerie familiarity. The scene before me looked like nothing so much as the Ebenezer Chapel of my Welsh home town. Varnished oak was the theme and there was the same overpowering stuffiness and damp. A dismal row of box pews faced me. Presumably the architect had in mind a phantom army of lawyers and journalists. I leaned back against the gothic wooden carving of a seat wide enough for two deacons.

"Is there still no sign of the deputy clerk?" I demanded of the keeper, anxious for some kind of reassurance.

"No sir."

"Well I suppose we'll simply have to manage on our own."

Mr. Perkins took up the case papers from the desk and shuffled off to the entrance hall. He returned with two ladies, both large and formidable in appearance.

"This" said Mr. Perkins, introducing the one on the right" is Mrs Elsie Brewster, sir. And this is her neighbour, Mrs Madge Daley. The two of them are charged with disorderly behaviour."

"Be seated on the front bench while I make a note" I told the parties "and watch my pen."

"I'm not sitting by 'er. Not for all the tea in China I'm not," declared Mrs Brewster.

"And me neither" said Mrs Daley.

This impasse was solved by placing Mrs Brewster in the witness box.

"How exactly did it all start?" I asked her.

"Well your worship" she said. "You'd think that being a wedding, Madge Daley would behave. Her Kevin marrying our Janice you see. They was standing in front of the parson and just as the preacher says 'If anyone knows of any lawful reason why this man and this woman should not be joined in holy matrimony speak or belt up' Madge Daley calls out 'JANICE BREWSTER'S A BLEEDIN LITTLE SCRUBBER!'

"That gave 'er no right to slag me with an umbrella," countered Mrs Madge Daley lumbering to her feet.

By now my writing had become totally unreadable, but Mrs Daley was already in full flood.

"Do you want to see the bruise, sir?"

She began to tug at her blouse, revealing an alarming pink undergarment.

"That won't be necessary Mrs Daley" I said.

I turned to Mr. Perkins. "What other evidence is there in this case?" He consulted the file.

"Well there's twenty three witnesses summonsed by Mrs Brewster and eighteen by Mrs Daley."

I felt one of my migraines coming on.

"Of course, sir" volunteered Mr. Perkins "in my early days, Mr. Cairns the Lambeth Magistrate was pretty successful with a Verse from the Scriptures in a domestic matter like this."

Knowledgably, he flicked open the court bible at an appropriate page.

It seemed to be worth a try.

"Both parties are to stand while I read from the Good Book," I said.

Adjusting my spectacles I peered at Psalm 113.

"Behold how pleasant it is for ye to dwell together in peace!" I began.

"Well that's good for a laugh" put in Mrs Brewster.

"It is like the precious oil upon the head" I read on.

"Oil!" exclaimed Mrs Daley. "I 'ad the whole effing wedding cake dropped on me head!"

I turned to Mr. Perkins in despair.

"No sir" he agreed "I don't think you've quite got the knack that Mr. Cairns had. Of course, he was a Methodist Preacher in his spare time."

Fortunately Mr. Perkins himself was able to persuade the truculent pair to be voluntarily bound over and I was able to move on to the next case.

"It's the other couple, sir," warned Keeper Perkins.

"Which two?"

"Mr. and Mrs Hurling, your worship. You can see from this load of papers that they've been hawking their matrimonial problems all around the courts of London for some time."

He plonked a bundle of dog-eared documents in front of me.

"Get sat down, Mrs Hurling" said Perkins "while Mr. Hurling takes the oath before his worship."

Mr. Hurling, it transpired, was a ledger-keeper with the Gas Board. A stooping bald-headed person, he had an unfortunate lisp.

"It's not that I'm wefusing to pay maintenance, sir" he told me "it's just that she's being totally unweasonable!"

"In what way is she unweasonable?" I enquired, "unreasonable," I added, hastily correcting myself.

"Well she decided she wanted to keep the pets sir."

"Well there's nothing wrong with that, surely."

"Well there is, sir, if they happen to be a pair of white wats."

"A pair of what, Mr. Hurling?"

"Wats" he squeaked with some irritation.

I paused to take this in.

"Well presumably she keeps the creatures in a cage, does she not?"

"Oh yes, she keeps the wats in a cage, except when she's giving them supper"

"Well a rat is entitled to supper Mr. Hurling" I pointed out.

"But not my supper sir."

I studied the case papers.

"I see from the application Mr. Hurling, that you have no family - you and your wife.

Perhaps Mrs Hurling is only keeping these rather strange pets out of a frustrated mother instinct."

"Well she must have a stwange mother-instinct, sir, if it's for two blinking wats."

I tried a new tack.

"Have you ever thought of starting a family, Mr. Hurling?" I enquired.

"Fat chance of that, sir, when she bwings the wats into the matwimonial bed."

At this point Mrs Hurling, a tiny bespectacled lady in strange knitted cap, jumped to her feet.

"It was only once I did that sir, and that was when it was a very cold night and the creatures would have frozen to death in their cage." She pulled a small pocket diary from her handbag. "What he hasn't told you about, sir, is his funny way over sex."

"Er, how do you mean?" I asked cautiously.

"I've kept a record of the dates, sir. He's got what our doctor calls a childhood regression, sir."

"And what form does that take Mrs Hurling?"

"He has to pretend that he's playing Cowboys and Indians, sir. He has to be the Indian."

Mr. Hurling was looking slightly bashful.

"All I do sir" he protested "is use a bit of warpaint, sir - the wife's lipstick - and put on my Indian headdress that I've had since boyhood sir."

"And you, Mrs Hurling?" I ventured.

"I have to wear this cowboy hat, and fire a toy pistol before he can get started sir" complained Mrs Hurling.

"I see."

"And if the cap in the gun is a dud, I have to say 'bang bang' sir."

I put down my pen and turned to Perkins.

"Does this court possess a copy of Pugh and Latey on Domestic Causes?" I enquired.

"Afraid not sir."

"Then I shall have to put this case over to enable the parties to consult an officer in the Inner London Marriage Guidance Service."

Back in Chambers, Mr. Perkins brought me a luke warm cup of tea.

"You see now what I mean" said Perkins. "Whenever the other courts come up against something that's going to take a long time to sort out, it's always the same story. 'Send it over to Lambeth' they say."   He offered me the last gingerbread biscuit, from a tin depicting the Coronation of King George Vth. "I'm sorry for you, sir, I really am. In fact I'm sorry for both of us."

"Now now Mr. Perkins" I said. "There's absolutely nothing to be gained by that sort of negative approach. One thing my wartime service in the artillery taught me, was to take the rough with the smooth."

"Well you'll certainly find the next case rough all right, sir," said Mr. Perkins. "You've got the inmates of the South London's Women's Hostel versus Major Riley (Royal Observer Corps Retired)."

It was late afternoon and already dusk. However, I was determined to press on and finish the day's work. The people involved in the earlier cases had stayed behind to watch me at work, from the public gallery, and I must not be seen a slacker.

"Call the case on" I told Perkins. "Let's hear what the ladies have to say."

"He's got this telescope, sir" explained their spokeswoman, an assertive blonde in a lime-green raincoat and white high-heels. "Has it to his eye in the window opposite. We can see him watching whenever we're undressing."

"I am an ornithologist, your worship" protested the Major "and I happen to be studying the urban migration of Barn Owls."   He saw the expression on my face and tried again. "I also endeavour to keep up on plane-spotting, my old expertise."

"Expertise!" exploded the complainant, "he's nothing but a Peeping Tom!"

"Well nobody's going to do much peeping around here" I said. "That's for sure."   The London Electricity Board had now succeeded in plunging us all into complete darkness. With the assistance of a match struck by Mr. Perkins, I managed to get safely back to the retiring room.

A telephone call to the Board confirmed that there was no chance of any resumption of supply that day.

"You'd better tell the parties that the case is remanded" I said. "They'll be notified when the matter is reinstated."

Just as I was about to leave, I encountered the missing Deputy Clerk. He had only then arrived and was conferring with Mr. Perkins, outside the main office.

"Very sorry to let you down, sir" he said "though I gather from Perkins that it's just been the usual round of S and M."

"S and M?"   I was trying to make my way down the steps in the evening gloom, the outside lights also having failed.

"Sex and Matrimonial. The routine performance."   He gave a feeble laugh. "Doing the Lambeth Walk, we call it. You'll soon pick it up."

"Watch that step, sir" called out a voice from the shadows, instantly recognizable as Mrs Brewster.

Too late.

The next minute, I was picking myself up from the pavement while Mr. and Mrs Hurling gathered together my papers. It seemed to be customary for the clients to give the magistrate a friendly send-off.

"Are you all right, sir?"   The D.C. handed me my bowler. "The council were supposed to have mended that last week."

"Tomorrow's another day sir" he said. Mr. Perkins hailed a taxi for me.

And another court, as far as I was concerned.

With the Lambeth Walk behind me I was soon to be summoned (as in the nursery rhyme, Oranges and Lemons) by the Bells of Shoreditch. Or more accurately by the Belles of Shoreditch.

CHAPTER SEVENTEEN

THE BELLES OF SHOREDITCH

"Henceforth" said Principal McVie's directive from Headquarters "the Domestic Court will comprise a Stipendiary Magistrate sitting with two lady J.P.s. Hearings to take place at the old County Court Building, Shoreditch."
Hector McVie was never one to welcome change.

"A Feminist Victory. if you ask me" he commented acidly, when I telephoned for details.

"One simply has to move with the times" I assured him. "I'm looking forward to meeting the ladies."

I was still in optimistic spirits when reporting for duty on the appointed day. There was a typed slip of paper from Mr. McVie waiting on the desk in the retiring room. This told me with whom I should be sitting: namely Councillor Audrey Gresham and the Honourable Penelope Brooke.

"Delighted to welcome you" I said, springing up to greet the first of my new colleagues to arrive.

She was carrying an enormous briefcase embossed Girton College, Cambridge.

"Can't think how one's managed in the past" I said. "It's difficult to adjudicate in family matters without the practical knowledge of a wife and mother."

"A wife I certainly am not, Mr. Knox Mawer" came the reply. She adjusted her rimless glasses more firmly above her Roman nose. "I shouldn't dream of saddling myself with one of your inadequate sex. And for the record, I am certainly not an unmarried mother."

"Oh, I wasn't suggesting Miss Gresham..."

"Professor Gresham please."

"Ah" I stammered. "What I really mean is that there's nothing like feminine intuition when assessing the credibility of evidence."

"If you mean rational thinking by a cool head" responded Professor Gresham "you might be on the right track."

Just then the usher shouted up to me through the open window. "The other lady J.P. is here sir, and wants to know where to park."

"There's plenty of room alongside mine" I called back. A loud screech of brakes accompanied by a metallic crunching noise followed.

"Seems you're wrong there sir" reported the usher.

I hurried outside. A large horsey woman peered out from the driving seat of a Range Rover which was fortunately undamaged. The steel mirror on my old Morris Minor was badly twisted.

"You've got that vehicle illegally parked in the space reserved for the Stipendiary Magistrate" complained the Honourable Penelope Brooke.

"I am the Stipendiary Magistrate, ma'am" I said.

Two huge German hunting dogs caged at the back of her vehicle were now pressed against the wire, baring their teeth at me in a distinctly unfriendly manner.

"They can always sense a nervous person" explained their owner.

I relieved the Honourable P.B. of her clipboard and followed on her heels as she strode into the Retiring Room.

"Why it's dear Audrey" exclaimed Penelope Brooke. She threw off an ancient hacking jacket and embraced the professor warmly. A distinct smell of manure arose from her leather boots.

"We're both on Reggie's Family Courts Advisory Committee" she observed, for my benefit.

"Reggie?"

"The Lord Chancellor, dear boy."

So far as my own career was concerned the Lord Chancellor was God.

She sifted through her papers on the clipboard.

"No doubt, Audrey" she said "Reggie wants us to make a full note as to how we get on today. It's something in the nature of an experiment after all!"

Nodding her head, Professor Gresham got out a black notebook from her briefcase.

"And of course, Mr. Knox Gore..."

"Mawer" I put in.

"Is very much a newcomer in the Family Court."

As we took our places upon the Bench I wiped the palms of my hands upon the blotter in front of me. It felt rather like being a Soviet dissident in between two members of the K.G.B.

Maintenance arrears occupied our first hour, with Professor Gresham conducting a most meticulous review of the household bills in each case. By the time we adjourned for lunch I was feeling pretty done-in.

"A little naive on the subject of home economics, aren't you?" chortled Penelope Brooke. "I suppose all those years of being waited on hand and foot in darkest Africa didn't help."

"The South Pacific" I began "and in point of..."

I was cut off mid-sentence by the loud snap of P.B's clipboard as she penned another entry, no doubt intended for the Lord Chancellor's Committee on the performance of the new Stipendiary Magistrate.

"You'd better read my own treatise on Home Spending Guidelines" added Professor Gresham, bringing out a substantial tome from her briefcase. "At least then I can tell Reggie you're making a beginning in that direction." She rummaged through the side flap and brought out more literature. "I also noticed one or two gaps in your knowledge of Child Benefit Allowances" she said. She smiled kindly. "If you don't mind my mentioning it."

I did.

All in all, my confidence had completely eroded by the time the afternoon session began.

"Horsepool v Horsepool" called our the listing officer.

Mr. Horsepool, a scraggy post office worker, was accused by his distinctly over-dressed wife of desertion, neglect and unreasonable behaviour. Evidence was given by both parties.

"If you ask me" hissed Professor Gresham "this husband is altogether lacking in responsibility. As Chairperson, you should be putting him through a proper grilling."

"Firm but fair is my approach" I murmured.

"Well you haven't even pressed him about Christmas Eve" reprimanded Professor Gresham. "He seemed to have left all the cooking entirely to his poor wife."

There was a sharp dig on my arm from the Honorable Penelope.

"You need to probe deeper about the reasons why he's been coming home so late," she insisted.

"Well he was working night shift on the Sorting Counter" I pointed out, "his wife's idea apparently."

"Well he certainly had no reason to object when his mother-in-law made a Yuletide visit, a bit of plain speaking from an older woman was just what was needed," said Professor Gresham.

"But surely she didn't have to polish off his only bottle of Christmas sherry?" I countered.

"Serves him right," said the Honorable P.B. "Otherwise we'd have had him up on a drunk and disorderly charge, no doubt."

And so it went on throughout the afternoon.

Harassed on both sides by my colleagues, I felt like somebody trapped in no-man's land. By the time the hearing had come to an end I could certainly be classed as a walking wounded if not a complete stretcher case.

Ensconced with my two colleagues in the Retiring Room I did my best to collect my thoughts on the case.

I myself was in favour of some sort of compromise ruling. According to the lady Justices however, Mr. Horsepool was solely to blame for everything. In the ensuing discussion my own reservations were crushed. I was in a minority of one, which meant a majority verdict against the hapless husband.

The defendant was duly informed of his fate. He steadied himself against the dock, before venturing a comment in a broken voice.

"What with the wife and the mother-in-law, you can't win sir" he said, lowering his voice confidentially. "Not, with respect, when you're got at by two women at the same time." He rolled his eyes in the direction of my two colleagues.

"Perhaps you'd agree with me, sir."

"That remark will be struck from the record" instructed the Honorable Penelope Brooke.

"Entirely irrelevant" agreed Professor Gresham.

Upon a sudden impulse, I spoke up.

"On the contrary" I said "I think the observation has considerable relevance. Let it stand."

With some satisfaction I rose and made my exit.

"The worm has turned" I murmured.

"Sorry sir?" The usher was still holding the Court Notebook.

"No. That's not for the record" I explained as I closed my Chamber's door," just a personal reminder."

CHAPTER EIGHTEEN

TOWER BRIDGE

When I rang the McVie Home there was silence at the other end of the line. Principal McVie was obviously not pleased to hear from me. The martinet was now, in his own words, "restoring order at Tower Bridge Court." It had been my unwelcome task to tell him that I was about to join him there. The regular magistrate had suddenly been taken ill.

"Indeed! Not a man of stamina I'm afraid," was McVie's response.

"Gone down to Bournemouth to recuperate" I explained "so Sir Robert says I must take his place."

I pictured Hector McVie adjusting his regimental tie-pin. He was the sort of man who dressed with military precision, as neatly off-duty as on.

"Trust you know the way" he barked, pulling himself together.

"Well, I was rather hoping you would lay on official transport."

"Out of the question" he replied.

"Unless you'd like the prison van diverted to pick you up!" he added caustically.

"It wouldn't be the first time" I told Mr. McVie, leaving him to puzzle that one out.

It had been one of my more memorable experiences in the Overseas Judiciary, some fifteen years earlier. My attendance had been urgently needed at Nalua, a remote township upon the eastern side of the Renai Estuary, which opens into Bligh Sound. I consulted Pandit Ram Shara, an equally memorable

Principal in his own way, as to how to get there. Mr. Shara was standing on his head at the time, the final position in the daily routine of his yoga exercises.

"Perhaps your honour would care to share the benefit of this relaxing posture while we discuss the problem" he suggested.

"Afraid there'll be no time today, Mr. Shara," I said "they need me at Nalua, as soon as is possible."

In the result, Pandit Shara proved far more co-operative than Principal McVie. He was good enough to drive me there himself. Nor was it his fault that his decrepit motorcar broke down in the sand en route, and we were obliged to hitch a lift in the first vehicle that came along. It was just bad luck that this turned out to be a lorry carrying twenty prisoners in their cage at the back.

Pandit Shara and I squeezed in beside the driver. We ignored the jeers and rattlings behind us and got to our destination safely enough. It was all part of the resourcefulness needed to cope with the unexpected in the outback of Empire.

With a rueful smile I brought myself back to the present as I concentrated on consulting the public transport section of the London A to Z. To get to the Tower Bridge Court, I took the eastbound underground route, but unfortunately disembarked on the wrong side of the Thames.

"This way to the Crown Jewels" called out a brisk lady guide, herding a crowd of Japanese tourists through the south side of the station exit.

"Turn right across the bridge, mate" said the helpful proprietor of a newspaper stand. "You'll find the court on the opposite side to your left."

I looked up at the black clouds rumbling in the sky. If I strode out smartly, I might perhaps make it in time, before the threatened rainstorm broke. I had done barely more than thirty yards onto the crossing when there was the warning sound of bells from the tower above my head. It was a startling experience. The tar macadam road in front of me divided and rose at an angle of about sixty-five degrees.

I rechecked my A to Z. It confirmed that Tower Bridge had long since ceased to open, now that the Pool of London was no longer used for berthing vessels. Why on earth should this happen to me, on the one day I needed to get across in a hurry!

"How long will the bridge be up?" I enquired of a burly official in a peaked cap, at the ground level entrance to the tower. "I've never heard of this happening before."

"We've never had a state visit by the Queen of the Netherlands before" he replied sharply.

As he spoke, a small warship flying the flag of the Royal Netherlands Navy steamed towards the bridge. The rest of his words were drowned in a barrage of gunfire.

The King's Troop of the Royal Artillery was firing a salute in Her Majesty's honour from the other side of Traitor's Gate. The Royal Dutch party could be seen acknowledging the tribute.

"Well that's that" I said as the V.I.P. vessel passed us by.

"Not exactly" the official personage told me with some relish. "Her Majesty is accompanied by six frigates of her navy, two of our own mine-sweepers and five high-masted cadet training-boats. About an hour, you might say."

I glanced at my watch. "This is an appalling emergency" I explained to Mr. Peaked Cap. "I'm the Tower Bridge Stipendiary Magistrate. Due to open court in five minutes time."

Slowly he took off his headgear and scratched his balding pate.

"Well it's not often the overhead footwalk is used" he said, doubtfully. He jerked a thumb upwards. Between the East and West Towers of the bridge, some seventy-five feet above our heads, the Victorian architect had constructed a walkway supported upon massive iron girders.

"There's no alternative" I declared.

"I wouldn't recommend it sir, not in this wind."

I waved aside his objections as he led me reluctantly into the creaking lift.

"Can't you wait at least until the storm has passed sir?" he suggested when letting me out at the top.

Heavy rain mixed with hailstones was pelting down on the walkway.

"Hold on, for God's sake, sir" were his last words as I plunged forwards on the long haul to the other side. This was sound advice, except that it meant losing my bowler hat. Nor was there anything I could do to stop my raincoat from billowing out. Indeed for a few anxious moments I was in grave danger of becoming completely airborne. As it was the wretched garment was caught on a spike in the iron railing. There was a loud ripping sound but I struggled onwards without it. By the time I reached the opposite tower, my court jacket and trousers were wet through. To my dismay I saw that there was nobody to operate the lift on that side. Instead I had to continue my descent along the winding staircase which was where somehow or other I lost my left shoe. Irretrievably as it happened. I watched it plunge downwards through a gap in the railing. There was nothing else to do, I decided, but press on, limping slightly as I reached street-level again.

Looming in front of me was the court-house itself, a building of impressive proportions with a marble entrance hall.

Perhaps under the circumstances I should have avoided the front entrance.

"Tell that dosser to go round to the jailer's office" called out the police officer on duty.

I was somewhat taken aback as I realised he was addressing me. A stern warrant officer with a list of Vagrancy Offenders in his hand started to hustle me along with the rest of the queue.

"Now look here, my good man" I began, assuming the functionary would recognise at least a faint note of authority in my voice, "if you'd been crossing the bridge on foot in weather like this -"

"Back in line there," was the response.

"This really is absurd, officer" I persisted.

I had removed my ruined overcoat and was drying my head with a handkerchief. There was nothing I could do about the missing shoe.

"The name is Knox Mawer" I continued "Metropolitan Stipendiary Magistrate, assigned to this court."

"Impersonating a magistrate is a very serious offence" he warned.

"That question does not arise" I replied. "I am the magistrate."

At last, the penny dropped. Perhaps he recognised my judicial tie, despite its condition.

With a profusion of apologies the bobby dropped his clipboard and led me to a door marked PRIVATE. A pair of shoes were found for me from a box marked FOR THE HOMELESS. They fitted me well enough for the time being.

"The matron will have your clothes dried out sir" he assured me as he led me along the corridor to my chambers. "And no doubt Principal McVie will be able to loan you a dry collar."

Unfortunately just at that moment, McVie himself emerged from his room.

"His worship was caught on top of Tower Bridge" explained the constable. "In the middle of the storm" he added, noting the Principal's expression of frozen disbelief.

"Entirely my own fault," I put in hastily, "throwing caution to the wind you might say."

"All too literally sir," he replied managing a smile. As I went on to explain in detail precisely what had happened I thought I detected a further unbending upon the part of McVie. Perhaps my determination in the face of adversity had sent me up in his estimation. He had, after all, been a Beach Commander in the Normandy landings.

"Better get you tidied up," he announced "before we press on."

In the result I was able to get through the day's Sitting without further difficulty.

"All's well that ends well," he conceded when I countersigned the Court Register late that afternoon. Perhaps I had made the grade at last.

CHAPTER NINETEEN

CRISIS AT KINGS CROSS

Word of my Tower Bridge adventure got back to H.Q.

"A rather unusual way to get to court" had been Sir Robert's comment, "but I must congratulate Knox Mawer upon his display of true British grit."

There was also a complimentary paragraph about me in the London Evening Standard. The headline read A BRIDGE TOO FAR. "The Beak Battles Through", the report went on.

It seemed I was the hero of the hour.

Flushed with triumph at this upturn in my career, my next move six months later, was to volunteer for an emergency sitting at the Kings Cross Neighbourhood Court, always a difficult posting on the London Circuit. It seemed that the elderly Resident Magistrate had cracked under the strain and eloped to Monte Carlo with a young lady police officer. There was left behind an urgent back-log of litigation.

"Stamina is what's needed in a job like this," I commented to Principal McVie who accompanied me to this notorious trouble spot. Mr. McVie looked alarmed. He had yet to adjust himself to the new Knox Mawer, hammer of the law.

"On your mark then, McVie," I said sotto voce as he announced my appearance in the court room. No sooner had I taken my place in the seat of justice than I took from my waistcoat pocket Father's gold Hunter watch.

"Right then" I said glancing up to check with the mahogany framed wall clock on the opposite wall. "let's see what we can get through before those hands come together." This was a favourite expression of Father's to indicate the hour of midday, always a crisis point in the workings of his High Street Emporium.

From the word go I had my customers at petty sessions bowling in and out like ninepins.

Applications were the first to be dealt with.

"Transfer of licence sanctioned"

"Protection order granted."

"Search warrant to issue."

It was then time for roll-call for those in the dock. Each case required a rapid assessment of the facts, a scrutiny of the papers, followed briskly by the necessary order. Speed was essential, although fair play remained the overriding motto - as I assured them all. They ranged from football hooligans, drug addicts, pornographers, to ladies of ill-repute.

"Attendance centre. Saturdays. 2-4, for 3 months."

"Sentence deferred. 18 months."

"Obscene books to be confiscated."

Work was proceeding at such a rate that even Mr. McVie could hardly keep pace as he handed up the charge sheets. Normally he prided himself on being the one who cracked the whip so to speak. On this occasion it was the other way round. Cases of pickpocketing alternated with joy-riding and assault.

"Imprisonment suspended for 2 years."

"Community Service Order."

"Summons and cross summons both proved.."

"Pretty good going" I said to myself as I glanced at the time. The clock showed 12.45 , so there was time for a quick spot of lunch.

My misbehaving predecessor had overlooked half a bottle of Madeira in his filing cupboard. I downed a tipple in a thermos-cup with my marmite sandwiches.

Mr. McVie declined the Madeira. "Not while on duty" was his grim reply, popping down an indigestion tablet as we resumed the sitting.

The first of the afternoon's traffic list concerned a Mr. Horace Spragg. He was guilty of careless driving.

"Far from stopping at the red light" explained the arresting constable "the defendant increased speed".

"I was trying to get to an urgent job" protested Mr. Spragg.

"Kindly hand up your driving licence for endorsement" I said.

He did this in such a hurry that he left his business card in the fold of the document.

H. SPRAGG FUNERAL DIRECTOR AND MORTICIAN it read, TWENTY FOUR HOUR SERVICE AROUND THE HOME COUNTIES. EMBALMING A SPECIALITY.

"That will be a £200 fine Mr. Spragg" I said. "Without the embalming!"

I leant over to Mr. McVie.

"Slip a note of my little wise crack to the Press Box," I directed "they'll like that one."

I was enjoying my newly found confidence. There was no hint of the hiatus that was ahead of me. Perhaps I should have detected the warning note in Mr. McVie's voice.

"You'll now have to try a Not Guilty plea under the new Traffic Act" he said "driving while over the limit of alcohol."

"Ah, ah" I replied casually.

"You'll be acquainted with the complications of the recent Breathalyser Regulations , no doubt?" he continued.

I nodded. In fact the details were entirely foreign to me. Traffic was hardly a problem amongst the atolls of the South Pacific where I had spent so many years. In Western Polynesia, "Funafuti 1" was the number on the Public Works Lorry, with less than a dozen ancient vehicles altogether. Toddy drinking on Vailevu merely produced torpor and there was only the single coast road around Nasese Bay. The bicycle taxis of Morea were incapable of more than 6 miles an hour.

"The issue that arises here" Principal McVie pointed out "is an important one. Was the defendant smoking at the time the officer required him to blow into the bag."

"Er yes."

" His worship will hear evidence from the police constable," directed Mr. McVie.

The P.C. explained that the suspect smelt of drink.

"I ordered him to give a puff before arresting him for excess alcohol." In answer to Mr. McVie, the constable conceded that the driver was enjoying a large cigar when apprehended.

Before the accused, a portly man in a camel court, took the stand. Mr. McVie seized the opportunity to probe my own expertise in the matter. He stepped behind his chair and leant his elbow on the bench, his face inches from mine. He began to grind his dentures, always a sign of renewed vigour. "Presumably sir, you're wholly familiar with the principles and operation of the equipment?" he said.

"Could be helpful to remind myself" I murmured.

"May I suggest that you study the Manufacturers Instructions on the lid" he persisted. "Alcotest 80 is the name of the apparatus."

With a flick of his finger he alerted the constable to the task in hand..

Solemnly the officer began the demonstration. He unwrapped and held up a tube containing some white crystals, at which point McVie took over.

"You'll know I hope, sir, that you have to scratch both ends of the ampoule, and break off the tip before inserting the green end into the collar of the bag."

"Ingenious" I murmured.

"And the white end goes into the mouth-piece,"

D.I.Y. has never been one of my strongest points. I must have been handling the ampoule rather carelessly. Somehow my finger slipped and there was a sound of fragmentation. In a trice a shower of crystals was discharged onto my lap. I stood up only to produce a crunching sound underfoot. This led to a powerful odour of some sort of chemical. The policeman sneezed loudly. There was a hastily smothered snigger from the Press Box..

"Case adjourned" I said, into my handkerchief. I brushed myself down as I made my bow.

"Until further evidence is heard."

Mr. McVie followed me into Chambers where he helped me into my mackintosh. A few stray crystals rolled from my cuff as I was buttoning up my waistcoat.

"You understand the position I hope Mr. McVie?"

"Crystal clear your worship" he replied with one of those maddening smiles of his.

Once again the Principal Chief Clerk had re-instated himself as Top Dog in our relationship.

CHAPTER TWENTY

A TARNISHED REPUTATION

The years that followed saw me settled into a fairly manageable routine. I had become interested in the history of the Metropolitan Courts, and often retreated after my sittings to the studious calm of the London Library to find out about the work of my illustrious predecessors.

Browsing there one afternoon in one of the dimly lit lower labyrinths I came across a series of articles in the Illustrated London News of 1908. Getting down the heavily-bound volume from the top shelf was something of a struggle. Fortunately a sturdy lady academic in a woollen cape was able to extricate me from the subsequent avalanche. But the contents of the volume made this little accident worth the effort. As I turned over the pages, the criminal world of the past rose vividly in my imagination.

There was one remarkable drawing captioned THE BROKEN-HEARTED PARENT. It depicted the horse-drawn Black Maria with a lady in a tattered shawl trying to persuade the constable to release a ferret-faced youth inside. Her son no doubt. In the background I recognised the familiar entrance to the cells at Tower Bridge Court.

An equally dramatic picture entitled THE PARADE showed a small child walking along a row of villainous-looking males in the yard of Bow Street Police Office, still largely unchanged in my time. The child points out the least likely suspect, a well dressed molester in a curly bowler hat. Another lithograph, captioned TRAGIC HAPPENING IN THE MORTUARY caught my eye. A uniformed sailor husband was identifying the body of his murdered wife who had evidently turned to prostitution. And there on the next page the Metropolitan Constabulary, under the direction of an officer on horseback were to be seen striking with raised truncheons at an unruly crowd. CALLOUS POLICE ATTACK ON PEACEABLE CROWD OUTSIDE LAMBETH COURT the story ran. The Stipendiary Magistrate had apparently been summoned to calm down the situation. I felt a glow of pride at the way my predecessors had dealt with these harrowing episodes of human tragedy. And now I myself was part of the story of crime and punishment in the heart of this Great City.

After a while I decided to take a rest from my studies. A short climb up the central red-carpeted stairs took me into the Reading Room where I was not exactly pleased to catch sight of a familiar figure. Austin Bolsover Q.C. was enjoying a post-prandial snooze in the best armchair.

"Long time no see dear boy," he exclaimed popping open his left eye "Still keeping the streets of London clean are we?!"

"You could put it that way," I said coolly.

I was perfectly aware that the Metropolitan Magistrates represented the bottom rung of the Judiciary. Even so my researches into their history did at least reveal 200 years of tradition.

It was more than could be said for V.A.T. Avoidance Loopholes which was Bolsover's legal speciality. "At least we don't give ourselves airs" I told him "like you and your fellow bloodsuckers in silk gowns!"

"That's just where you're wrong" said Austin rousing his portly frame from the chair. "London Beaks are the most pompous lot of all. Let me remind you of a few examples."

He lumbered over to a nearby reference shelf, bringing back an assortment of biographical dictionaries.

"See what this entry, for instance, has to say about one of your predecessors EC Boyd.

'Without question all who experienced his supercilious manner found him insufferable' ".

"He was clearly an exception" I said.

"Nonsense. Anybody who has had a brief before Rowley Thomas will tell you that he was a complete megalomaniac. Literally used to jump up and down in his chair when indignant, which he usually was. Always referred to foreigners as rotters or cads."

"Probably a gross exaggeration" I said "at least Rowley Thomas had the reputation of always saying what he thought."

"That was because he was never sober" said Bolsover. He gave me a playful punch in the chest. "Nothing personal old sport but he certainly gave you Taffies an unfortunate name on the Metropolitan Bench."

"Nonsense" I said "what about the famous Daniel Hopkin M.P. Universally popular. Rose from a humble Glamorgan -shire background too. A splendid addition to the London Magistracy."

"That's as maybe" said Austin "but he did not live long enough to undo the damage done by Welsh stipes like Cedric Powell . Always smelt of onions. Or Anstruther Merrick with his so-called witticisms."

"Well at least he made the headlines."

"Yes usually for his indiscretions."

"You're only jealous because nobody has even heard of your existence. Buried alive under your wretched tax cases."

"What makes you proud of such predecessors as Thomas de Veil the sex maniac, George Norton the blackmailer and Alan Laing the odious model for Charles Dickens's Mr. Fang!"

Austin was now in full spate, red jowls quivering.

"Those figures come from the remote past" I said. "Amongst hundreds of sound apples there are bound to be one or two not up to scratch."

"How would you have felt to be in the hands of a Beak who had clung to office until he was nearly 90?"

"Presumably you're referring to Mr. Frederick Mead. He retained his faculties 'til the last."

"If that was so why did he bully the first women police constables in such a persistent manner?"

"A person of his seniority was entitled to a few eccentricities," I said. "Particularly when his job at Marlborough Street was so demanding."

I dug into my briefcase and pulled out some dog-eared notes from my file.

"Here's a good summing-up of the problems facing the Marlborough Street Beak. Taken out of the Illustrated London News again."

I put on my reading spectacles.

"In Great Marlborough Street" I read "all kinds of persons of all degrees of society rub shoulders together; here extremes meet with a vengeance. Peers and pickpockets, members of parliament and members of the swell mob, the army, the navy and the bar, leading figures from literature and the fine arts, representatives of all the clubs in Pall Mall."   I chuckled. "Probably your own club included" I observed.

"Nobody's disputing that Marlborough Street has deserved a good Beak. But that's just the point. As The Times said recently it's for that very reason that it has been the graveyard of more than one magisterial reputation."

"And the making of many others," I pointed out. "Take John Hardwick for instance. In his day the London stipendiaries were under constant attack from reformers. But nobody had a bad word to say for him."

I flicked to the relevant entry in one of the dictionaries of national biography on a shelf by Bolsover's feet.

'Hardwick was universally popular on the Bench. Everywhere noted for his curtesy and linguistic ability. He conducted court business in an easy and conversational but by no means undignified style.'

I was about to read on when I was interrupted by an angry snort from the table behind me.

An elderly scholar was rustling his papers with considerable testiness. "Is the rule for silence totally ignored these days?" he demanded. It was not the first time for me to make this particular mistake.

Austin and I tiptoed hastily out onto the red carpeted main stairway.

"Methinks I hear from afar the tinkle of ice in a glass" said Bolsover. He was referring of course to the white-coated barman setting up drinks in the nearby Ritz Hotel one of his favourite haunts.

"You'll join me of course."

The thought of returning a round in that prohibitively expensive hotel made me blink.

"Isn't there somewhere a bit further afield where prices are reasonable?" I demurred.

Within a trice Bolsover had hailed a cab. "My friend wants you to take us to the cheapest dive in the East End," he guffawed over the driver's shoulder.

"Know the very place, gov.", came the response.

It was useless to argue but I quailed in despair when we drew up at the Kings Head in Old Street, E.1.

"For god's sake Bolsover" I protested "there was an affray in this very place only last week. It came before me on the Bench in heaven's name!"

It so happened that I had been doing a stint at Old Street Court that particular month.

"Then you'll enjoy seeing a bit of low life for yourself my old China," he replied leading the way into the saloon bar.

I have a poor head for alcohol and usually restrict myself to orange juice. This time though I felt in need of fortification and ordered a sherry. Austin Bolsover meanwhile insisted upon an enormous glass of whisky and was soon exchanging toasts with the criminal fraternity of Bishopsgate. After a while his eye was caught by one of the pub's ornaments - a stuffed bird in a glass cage.

"How much for the pheasant?" he demanded of the landlord.

"It's yours for 50 quid mate."

"Done" said Austin, slapping down five ten-pound notes.

About an hour later we were standing outside hoping to spy a taxi.

"Just hold onto this for a minute," said Austin retiring into the gent's loo.

By this time I had surrendered my tie to one of Austin Bolsover's more aggressive drinking companions.

"Where did you nick that from?" enquired a passing constable in a jokey mood. He was referring to the glass-cased trophy in my hand.

"My friend paid the owner fifty pounds for it, officer" I said.

"Tell that to the old bugger on the Bench," observed the bobby with a wink.

"He **is** the old bugger on the Bench" said Austin, reappearing alongside us.

He quickly put the amused constable in the picture before waving another taxi to a halt.

For my part I reckoned it would be more prudent to take the nearest tube. Bolsover climbed in behind the cabbie and placed his purchase on his lap.

"Should impress the customers in our Chambers," he said through the window.

"Unless you'd like him for Marlborough Street. Another stuffed Beak on the Bench!" he called back with a final wave.

Head down I slowly made my way to the Underground Station. Like the King's Head the London Library was a place to be avoided from now on. Especially any Saturday afternoon in the Reading Room

CHAPTER TWENTY ONE

COUNTING THE COST

The irksome Bolsover was only one source of trouble. A far more persistent fly in the ointment was of course Hector McVie, whose Gestapo-like presence had been so unnerving in my day-to-day life. Miraculously he had disappeared from the scene. My relief can be imagined when told that he had been seconded by Whitehall to the Police Disciplinary Authority in Great Smith Street SW1. Apparently an iron-willed Chief Executive was needed at the helm. Mr. McVie fitted the bill perfectly.

Without my dreaded Court Principal forever hustling me along, I was able to organise work to allow me a little more leisure-time. As a result my research into Metropolitan Legal History was proving to be an enjoyable hobby.

But when I look back I wonder whether I perhaps allowed myself too much spare time. I had always been a worrier, and now the various diseases contracted during my Tropical Service began to prey on my free-ranging imagination. All too soon I became a regular customer at the Albert Schweitzer Institute of Equatorial Pathology.

"We don't need more than one specimen of urine per week Mr. Knox-Mawer," said Professor Hindley.

"I thought you might detect traces of the Malubai Syndrome by means of a daily check," I protested.

He smiled and shook his head.

It was all very well for the Professor to dismiss my concern. He himself had never contracted this particular scourge of so many of us Servants of Empire.

His scepticism merely made me more determined than ever to keep a keen lookout on my physical condition in every possible manner.

I happened to be questioning the Medical Assessor in an Insurance Fraud trial at Thames Court one morning when I thought I detected a rise in my temperature. The curious hot flushes that now assailed me could surely not be explained away by the recent overhaul of the boiler directly under the Bench. I decided to bring a thermometer to Chambers and keep a record throughout the hearing. This naturally entailed constant adjournments, but it was better to err on the cautious side.

I was convinced that further checks were necessary. Some people might flinch from the anaesthetist's needle to take a blood sample. Not in my case however. I had too often been subject to the attentions of the voracious Royal Fruit Bats in Vailevu. These imperial pets often invaded my bedroom whenever I paid a judicial visit to King Tombi's palace.

"That's eight blood samples you've had us take in four days" cautioned the Senior Consultant at the Kitchener Laboratory. "And there's absolutely no sign whatsoever of this Papuan Liver Worm you keep mentioning."

"Better safe than sorry," was my reply.

That very evening I telephoned J.S. at his Yorkshire number. I wanted to know if my memory was serving me right, and he was an old hand where unhealthy climates were involved.

"Just caught me in time, old boy" he said "I'm off back to the South Seas. Can't stand these bloody moors in the winter any longer. Going to run a coconut plantation on Taivalu."

"Do you remember the medical term for that wretched sand gnat of the Loloma Isles? The one who's bite caused a nasty fever?"

"Never had trouble with it whatsoever dear chap" he replied. He snorted irascibly. "Surely you're not up to your old hypochondriac tricks? Thought I'd cured you of all that nonsense. Anyway it's probably all to do with your present regime - endless commuting, junk food and so on. Do you have to live out in the sticks at the Elephant and Castle?"

"It happens to be Wimbledon."

"Why on earth didn't you stay at the centre of things in my Soho flat?"

"I'm surprised you should mention that awful place after the trouble there."

"No trouble whatsoever my lad. Told the authorities I had Diplomatic Immunity and they tore up the court papers right away." He let out a chortle.

Fortunately it was impossible to bear a grudge against J.S. for long. We were soon chatting amiably about former times.

"Surely you know that I've always suffered from a weak constitution," I told him. "We can't all enjoy your rude health."

"You could if you kept away from those damned doctors. As ever your ailments are purely imaginary, Sunny Jim. Just lie back with a stiff whisky and let the bubbles of your mind float to the surface."

I groaned.

"You know how ill you made me, J.S. with your Scotch Grouse at the Planters Club that Christmas Eve."

He ignored this.

"Mind over matter," he chuntered. "The Orientals always have the answer. I'll put something in the post for you."

He was as good as his word. Two days later a curry-stained newspaper cutting fell out of a recycled envelope from J.S. THE ROAD TO HEALTHY LIVING the cutting read. "Learn to practise Transcendental Meditation at the School of Alternative Medicine."

Upon an impulse I made the necessary phone call. The following week, for a down-payment of twenty pounds, Mr. Kai Ling welcomed me into his dimly lit consulting-room off the Edgeware Road. I was evidently enrolled upon his course.

"Most fortunate" he told me "we're having a long waiting list."

There was no sign of any other patients that I could see.

A highly coloured photograph of Mr. Kai in a mortar board and some kind of Tibetan robe was framed on his desk.

"O.K. First we have to lelax."

"Certainly" I agreed, only too eager to relax. I made for the worn-out couch in the corner but Mr. Kai looked stern.

"On the floor please. Lie flat and lemove shoes and socks."

Nervously I complied. Mr. Kai slipped on a white jacket, the sort associated with dentists. From the pocket he took out a small hammer. I flinched, remembering the back tooth I had broken over breakfast. To my relief he proceeded to tap the soles of my feet.

"Lefflexology" he explained.

It took me a moment to puzzle this one out but Mr. Kai had already moved on to the next stage of treatment.

"Lib cage" said Mr. Kai.

"Sorry?"

He indicated the side of his chest. "Let out air in lib cage".

"Can I breathe again" I gasped.

"Why not" said Mr. Kai breezily. He popped a wad of chewing gum into his mouth.

"Now comes hypnothelapy."

I don't know quite how it happened. As my eyes followed the silver medallion which he swung to and fro over my head I seemed to go into a sort of coma. Dimly I was aware of Mr. Kai repeating a strange incantation. It should have been a peaceful experience. Unfortunately when I woke up I was in a cold sweat and firmly convinced that I had become Hector McVie.

"What's the time?!" I gabbled. "Court sitting is fifty seconds late already!"

I struggled to fasten my collar. Mr. Kai laid a soothing hand on my brow. Only a strong infusion of his valerian herbal tea brought me back to my senses.

"Tension gone" said Mr. Kai. "Personality conflict resolved. OK   Better now. Bye bye."

I scrambled to my feet still in a state of confusion. "Am inducing strength of character."

"Thank you very much" I gasped, dabbing at the beads of sweat on my forehead. "Do I need another appointment?"

"Not necessary" said Mr. Kai. "But I give you your mantla for daily use. Open mouth and say oom aaaah".

I had a go. Mr. Kai seemed satisfied as he waved me away. "Will calm conflict and help tension."

Sadly I did not seem to be the sort of patient that Mr. Kai could help. His herbal tea gave me a wholly sleepless night and when I tried repeating the mantra in chambers that afternoon Mrs Arnold the homely court matron enquired whether I was suffering from lockjaw.

It must have been about a month later that I was descending the stairs on a number 88 double decker. Suddenly the driver braked sharply and I was unable to keep my balance. By the time of my next appointment with Professor Hindley at the

Schweitzer Institute I had been fitted with a surgical collar and knee-brace.

The professor was far from sympathetic. "A very good thing" he pronounced cheerily. "Now you have a few genuine aches and pains to worry about, your chronic anxiety condition will disappear. You'll see."
I am afraid he was wrong.

CHAPTER TWENTY TWO

CURTAIN CALL

All too soon a host of fresh anxieties had materialised. My tropical ailments were more or less under control and I had dispensed with the collar and brace. However a new dilemma was upon me. The burning question was this. Was I fit enough to retire?

This problem had arisen because of a Whitehall Circular. Due to Government Cutbacks, early retirement was on offer for those of us who felt ready to go. Was I ready? And where would I go?

The second question was more easily answered than the first. Obviously I would go to the remote family cottage in Wales bought for a song some years earlier.

I prevaricated over the first question until I suddenly came to one of my snap decisions. Yes I was ready to retire. After all I had carried my burden of judicial office to the farthest outposts of Empire and latterly back home in our Great Metropolis itself. I had done my best. Now came the moment for me to make my exit.

Father's favourite piece of Tennyson sprang to mind.
    "Let there be no moaning at the Bar as I depart" were the words fitted by me (rather wittily I thought) into my speech at the farewell gathering in my honour.
    "You'll certainly be remembered" agreed Sir Robert Mildmay, downing a distinctly third-rate glass of hock. Mr. McVie was unable to attend. He did, nevertheless, send me a letter in his cramped handwriting. "We've had our differences"

he wrote. "On the other hand I am confident we bear no grudges one to the other."

I was not too sure about that. "As you know" his note concluded "I'm a keen fly fisherman.. Usually I go to Scotland. Who knows, one day it may be Wales."

"Retiring gracefully?", inquired the highly-coloured leaflet which arrived for me a few weeks later. It had been dropped in the bread bin, my makeshift letterbox at our hillside cottage near Llangollen. "Let us help you make the choice."   A shower of similar brochures followed, depicting   rosey-cheek, silver-haired pensioners gliding past their dahlias aboard a motor-mower, ascending the stairs by comfy chair-lift, springing from an orthopaedic bed to greet the happy dawn. This approach was new to me. Like Father (subconsiously probably hero-worshipped by me) I was sticking to a spartan mattress in more or less arctic conditions.

Prominent amongst the Senior Citizens Literature delivered to my door was a pamphlet headed "Share your Experience of Life as a public lecturer". I was not at all keen on the idea. However I was persuaded to appear at the local Church Missionary Bazaar.

"Ladies and gentlemen" said the vicar "our guest speaker is my friendly neighbour Ronnie Knox-Mawer."

Friendly was just how I was not feeling towards the vicar. In the first place, he had got me there under false pretences.

"An ideal opportunity to launch your book" was how he put it.

The book in question was a series of reminiscences about my judicial career in the South Seas. It had been based on the notes once spotted with marked disapproval in my brief case by Principal McVie himself.

I had already sat for twenty minutes while the vicar rambled on about various parochial events, without making any mention whatsoever of my book. Worse still, although I had sent six large cartons, each containing twelve copies of my memoirs to the Church Hall, there was not a single one to be seen, either on the platform or in any other part of the hall. Nor had the vicar pointed out the significance, let alone the reason, for my appearance. After all the Pacific Islanders had been a fertile ground for missionary work in earlier years.

"The audience will be disappointed if you don't bring along a few interesting trophies" the vicar had said. So I had taken him at his word, and equipped myself with a case of exhibits to conjure up the right atmosphere.

A central episode in the book described the occasion when the Valoma Islanders had made me an honorary Village Elder. So I began my address with a demonstration, holding up the Bird of Paradise feathers to my brow, the adornment I had worn at the ritual ceremony. This re-enactment on my part proved to be a mistake. To be frank, for someone who had held High Judicial Office in Oceania, it was a little demeaning to hear a sniggering choirboy at the back refer to me as "Big Chief Paleface." Nor did it help when I donned a Polynesian war-mask to be greeted with the amused cry "Batman!"

"The talk I am giving tonight" I proceeded, once the audience had settled down again "will, I trust, show that our great system of British Justice is adaptable to every corner of the globe, however remote. Naturally I shall concentrate upon my own work in those tiny outposts of Empire."

I had already installed the necessary projector and screen and was ready with the first of my slides.

"The treatment of Young Offenders Ordinance" I began, "was a measure I myself introduced in Lomoa, and this you see on the screen is the bamboo probation office erected at Sabu Sabu under my direction. Or rather it will be, when I get the slide the right way up."

From the back of the hall I thought I detected a somewhat impatient rattle of teacups as I was making the necessary adjustment.

"Now there" I continued, inserting slide two "is the Papalangi Community Service Canoe."

From Papalangi, I moved on to a couple of slides showing myself on horseback during an up-country safari in New Guinea. Some of these were out of focus, and it was not altogether easy to distinguish myself from my trusty steed, a broken down beast belonging to the island witch-doctor.

Looking back I can see perhaps I did have too many slides in my collection, particularly of the Community Service Centre Taki-raki and the Open-air Reformatory, Sabu Sabu. In fact, as I was explaining the Melanesian Spent Conviction Order-in-Council, I detected a falling-off of attention amongst my listeners. An elderly woman in the third row had fallen asleep, while her companion had taken out her knitting and was busy counting stitches.

"I shall just turn off the lights while I disconnect the plug of the Projector, ladies and gentlemen" I explained. I had not realised how narrow was the platform upon which I was speaking. I stepped back in the dark and was disconcerted to discover myself upside down in a crumpled heap, against the back-cloth for the Christmas pantomime, Jack and the Beanstalk. I quickly pulled myself together.

"Just bear with me one moment, please" I called up. The microphone lead had come down with me and was entangled with some cardboard cut-out of Gnomes and Elves. I fumbled for my handkerchief. A flake of war paint had come off the Polynesian mask and lodged itself in my eye, causing it to water badly. The vicar's concerned face loomed above mine. "Come on, man. No need for tears. Accidents happen to everyone."

Somewhat surprised, I got up, brushed myself down and was soon back at the podium, my usual calm and collected self. The sympathetic chuckles died away.

"Perhaps that little incident" I told the gathering "actually emphasises the point I wish to make. Namely that it is Quick Thinking that gains respect amongst people the world over. Adaptability is the trick. A rapid response in every unexpected crisis."

At the conclusion of this, my final peroration, I sat down to somewhat muted applause.

Just as the vicar was moving the usual vote of thanks, there was an interruption from the gallery.

"I wish to second the vote of thanks" called out a loud female voice "I happen to know the speaker and can say that at least there's no side to him, despite his being what he says he was".

My heart sank. I immediately recognised the lady speaker as Mair the waitress from my favourite eating-place in Froncysllte.

"He's the fella that likes to come into our little Empire Cafe for his brunch every day. He has two fried eggs and one jumbo sausage. His own bottle of tomato ketchup is kept specially for him in the cupboard. The Breakfast Man, we call him."

Unfortunately Mair's information aroused the audience into a state of lively interest. And she had, of course, been telling no less than the truth. It was my habit to escape each day to where I was hopefully unknown, in order to work upon my memoirs incognito. Incognito no longer alas!   All formality was gone. My judicial persona had been abruptly shattered.

"What we can never understand" added the speaker, enjoying the curiosity around her "is how you make one tea bag last for five cups." Roars of laughter greeted this sally.

"Well" said the vicar "it is usual for our speaker to answer questions. Are there any others?"

"Yes" volunteered the same lady in the gallery "could you tell us whether the book you've written is the one you were making all those notes for in the cafe? The ones you spilt the ketchup on, remember?"

I indicated to the vicar that I had no wish to open up a discussion upon my personal domestic routine. But by now the enquiries were coming in thick and fast.

"How different had breakfast been in the tropics?" an amateur anthropologist asked "yams, bananas and so on...?"

"How many bottles of sauce do you get through in a week?"

"Why didn't you write in the library instead of the Empire Cafe?"

"How on earth did you concentrate with the usual juke box they have playing in the corner?"

"Hemingway wrote in a cafe in Paris" volunteered the young local assistant librarian on the end of the first row. "Had he influenced your work?"

I did my best. By the time the evening came to an end, I was a nervous wreck. By the side door, I glimpsed a pile of my books on top of the missing boxes. A few people were picking them and putting them down again.

"Well thank you very much, Mr. Knox Mawer" said the vicar, as he saw me off at the door. "I shall look forward to seeing you at the usual time, next Sunday morning. We're delighted to have you as an additional sidesman. By the way, how do we refer to you in our parish magazine. Your proper official title, now that you're retired?"

I thought for a moment then gave up.

"Just call me The Breakfast Man" I said.

It was Mair who had the bright idea of selling the books at the restaurant.

Our little part of Wales has become a centre for the tourist trade, especially for Americans doing a package tour of the Principality and my slim volume of memoirs seems to have become a sort of addition to the menu. If I'm on hand, I'm only too happy to sign a copy for the visitors.

"Gee, such a sad story" said one of them, shaking his head. "Sent away from your own country. Living in exile all those years."

"And that Tom Jones song" suggested a friend. "When you come home again to Wales."

"Do you know it?"

"Can you sing it?"

The leader of the group wanted to know if my mountain cottage was on their coach itinerary. "I'll certainly be telling the Welsh Tourist Board about this. An old curiosity such as yourself should definitely be on the Cymric Heritage Trail" were his parting words as I made my escape

Nearby my cottage is a stream with a notice EXCELLENT FLY FISHING. A nightmare thought has struck me. What if Principal McVie should make his threatened appearance with his anglers tackle........?

Time to be on the move again I feel. Whether coming or going does not really matter anymore.